THE
COMANCHE

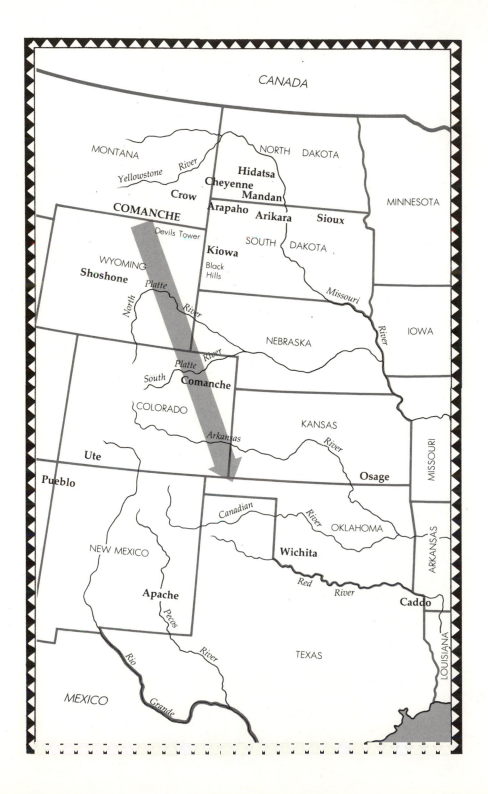

THE
COMANCHE

Willard H. Rollings
Southwest Missouri State University

Frank W. Porter III
General Editor

CHELSEA HOUSE PUBLISHERS
New York   Philadelphia

On the cover Comanche woman's boots, 1870, made from dyed leather, decorated with rawhide fringe, glass beads, and German-silver buttons. Courtesy of Denver Art Museum.

Chelsea House Publishers

Editor-in-Chief Nancy Toff
Executive Editor Remmel T. Nunn
Managing Editor Karyn Gullen Browne
Copy Chief Juliann Barbato
Picture Editor Adrian G. Allen
Art Director Maria Epes
Manufacturing Manager Gerald Levine

Indians of North America

Senior Editor Marjorie P. K. Weiser

Staff for **THE COMANCHE**

Deputy Copy Chief Ellen Scordato
Editorial Assistant Claire Wilson
Assistant Art Director Loraine Machlin
Designer Donna Sinisgalli
Design Assistant James Baker
Picture Researcher Ann Bohlen
Production Coordinator Joseph Romano

3 5 7 9 8 6 4

Library of Congress Cataloging-in-Publication Data

Rollings, Willard H.
The Comanche / Willard H. Rollings.
p.   cm.—(Indians of North America)
Bibliography: p.
Includes index.
Summary: Examines the culture, history, and changing fortunes of the Comanche Indians.
ISBN 1-55546-702-4.
      0-7910-0359-0 (pbk.)
1. Comanche Indians—Juvenile Literature. [1. Comanche Indians. 2. Indians of North America.] I. Title. II. Series: Indians of North America (Chelsea House Publishers)
E99.C85R65 1989   88-33987
973'.0497—dc19   CIP
                                          AC

CONTENTS

INDIANS OF NORTH AMERICA

CHELSEA HOUSE PUBLISHERS

INDIANS OF NORTH AMERICA: CONFLICT AND SURVIVAL

Frank W. Porter III

*The Indians survived our open intention of wiping them out, and
since the tide turned they have even weathered our good intentions
toward them, which can be much more deadly.*

John Steinbeck
America and Americans

When Europeans first reached the North American continent, they found hundreds of tribes occupying a vast and rich country. The newcomers quickly recognized the wealth of natural resources. They were not, however, so quick or willing to recognize the spiritual, cultural, and intellectual riches of the people they called Indians.

The Indians of North America examines the problems that develop when people with different cultures come together. For American Indians, the consequences of their interaction with non-Indian people have been both productive and tragic. The Europeans believed they had "discovered" a "New World," but their religious bigotry, cultural bias, and materialistic world view kept them from appreciating and understanding the people who lived in it. All too often they attempted to change the way of life of the indigenous people. The Spanish conquistadores wanted the Indians as a source of labor. The Christian missionaries, many of whom were English, viewed them as potential converts. French traders and trappers used the Indians as a means to obtain pelts. As Francis Parkman, the 19th-century historian, stated, "Spanish civilization crushed the Indian; English civilization scorned and neglected him; French civilization embraced and cherished him."

Nearly 500 years later, many people think of American Indians as curious vestiges of a distant past, waging a futile war to survive in a Space Age society. Even today, our understanding of the history and culture of American Indians is too often derived from unsympathetic, culturally biased, and inaccurate reports. The American Indian, described and portrayed in thousands of movies, television programs, books, articles, and government studies, has either been raised to the status of the "noble savage" or disparaged as the "wild Indian" who resisted the westward expansion of the American frontier.

Where in this popular view are the real Indians, the human beings and communities whose ancestors can be traced back to ice-age hunters? Where are the creative and indomitable people whose sophisticated technologies used the natural resources to ensure their survival, whose military skill might even have prevented European settlement of North America if not for devastating epidemics and disruption of the ecology? Where are the men and women who are today diligently struggling to assert their legal rights and express once again the value of their heritage?

The various Indian tribes of North America, like people everywhere, have a history that includes population expansion, adaptation to a range of regional environments, trade across wide networks, internal strife, and warfare. This was the reality. Europeans justified their conquests, however, by creating a mythical image of the New World and its native people. In this myth, the New World was a virgin land, waiting for the Europeans. The arrival of Christopher Columbus ended a timeless primitiveness for the original inhabitants.

Also part of this myth was the debate over the origins of the American Indians. Fantastic and diverse answers were proposed by the early explorers, missionairies, and settlers. Some thought that the Indians were descended from the Ten Lost Tribes of Israel, others that they were descended from inhabitants of the lost continent of Atlantis. One writer suggested that the Indians had reached North America in another Noah's ark.

A later myth, perpetrated by many historians, focused on the relentless persecution during the past five centuries until only a scattering of these "primitive" people remained to be herded onto reservations. This view fails to chronicle the overt and covert ways in which the Indians successfully coped with the intruders.

All of these myths presented one-sided interpretations that ignored the complexity of European and American events and policies. All left serious questions unanswered. What were the origins of the American Indians? Where did they come from? How and when did they get to the New World? What was their life—their culture—really like?

In the late 1800s, anthropologists and archaeologists in the Smithsonian Institution's newly created Bureau of American Ethnology in Washington,

D.C., began to study scientifically the history and culture of the Indians of North America. They were motivated by an honest belief that the Indians were on the verge of extinction and that along with them would vanish their languages, religious beliefs, technology, myths, and legends. These men and women went out to visit, study, and record data from as many Indian communities as possible before this information was forever lost.

By this time there was a new myth in the national consciousness. American Indians existed as figures in the American past. They had performed a historical mission. They had challenged white settlers who trekked across the continent. Once conquered, however, they were supposed to accept graciously the way of life of their conquerors.

The reality again was different. American Indians resisted both actively and passively. They refused to lose their unique identity, to be assimilated into white society. Many whites viewed the Indians not only as members of a conquered nation but also as "inferior" and "unequal." The rights of the Indians could be expanded, contracted, or modified as the conquerors saw fit. In every generation, white society asked itself what to do with the American Indians. Their answers have resulted in the twists and turns of federal Indian policy.

There were two general approaches. One way was to raise the Indians to a "higher level" by "civilizing" them. Zealous missionaries considered it their Christian duty to elevate the Indian through conversion and scanty education. The other approach was to ignore the Indians until they disappeared under pressure from the ever-expanding white society. The myth of the "vanishing Indian" gave stronger support to the latter option, helping to justify the taking of the Indians' land.

Prior to the end of the 18th century, there was no national policy on Indians simply because the American nation has not yet come into existence. American Indians similarly did not possess a political or social unity with which to confront the various Europeans. They were not homogeneous. Rather, they were loosely formed bands and tribes, speaking nearly 300 languages and thousands of dialects. The collective identity felt by Indians today is a result of their common experiences of defeat and/or mistreatment at the hands of whites.

During the colonial period, the British crown did not have a coordinated policy toward the Indians of North America. Specific tribes (most notably the Iroquois and the Cherokee) became military and political pawns used by both the crown and the individual colonies. The success of the American Revolution brought no immediate change. When the United States acquired new territory from France and Mexico in the early 19th century, the federal government wanted to open this land to settlement by homesteaders. But the Indian tribes that lived on this land had signed treaties with European governments assuring their title to the land. Now the United States assumed legal responsibility for honoring these treaties.

At first, President Thomas Jefferson believed that the Louisiana Purchase contained sufficient land for both the Indians and the white population. Within a generation, though, it became clear that the Indians would not be allowed to remain. In the 1830s the federal government began to coerce the eastern tribes to sign treaties agreeing to relinquish their ancestral land and move west of the Mississippi River. Whenever these negotiations failed, President Andrew Jackson used the military to remove the Indians. The southeastern tribes, promised food and transportation during their removal to the West, were instead forced to walk the "Trail of Tears." More than 4,000 men, woman, and children died during this forced march. The "removal policy" was successful in opening the land to homesteaders, but it created enormous hardships for the Indians.

By 1871 most of the tribes in the United States had signed treaties ceding most or all of their ancestral land in exchange for reservations and welfare. The treaty terms were intended to bind both parties for all time. But in the General Allotment Act of 1887, the federal government changed its policy again. Now the goal was to make tribal members into individual landowners and farmers, encouraging their absorption into white society. This policy was advantageous to whites who were eager to acquire Indian land, but it proved disastrous for the Indians. One hundred thirty-eight million acres of reservation land were subdivided into tracts of 160, 80, or as little as 40 acres, and allotted tribe members on an individual basis. Land owned in this way was said to have "trust status" and could not be sold. But the surplus land—all Indian land not allotted to individuals—was opened (for sale) to white settlers. Ultimately, more than 90 million acres of land were taken from the Indians by legal and illegal means.

The resulting loss of land was a catastrophe for the Indians. It was necessary to make it illegal for Indians to sell their land to non-Indians. The Indian Reorganization Act of 1934 officially ended the allotment period. Tribes that voted to accept the provisions of this act were reorganized, and an effort was made to purchase land within preexisting reservations to restore an adequate land base.

Ten years later, in 1944, federal Indian policy again shifted. Now the federal government wanted to get out of the "Indian business." In 1953 an act of Congress named specific tribes whose trust status was to be ended "at the earliest possible time." This new law enabled the United States to end unilaterally, whether the Indians wished it or not, the special status that protected the land in Indian tribal reservations. In the 1950s federal Indian policy was to transfer federal responsibility and jurisdiction to state governments, encourage the physical relocation of Indian peoples from reservations to urban areas, and hasten the termination, or extinction, of tribes.

Between 1954 and 1962 Congress passed specific laws authorizing the termination of more than 100 tribal groups. The stated purpose of the termination policy was to ensure the full and complete integration of Indians into American society. However, there is a less benign way to interpret this legislation. Even as termination was being discussed in Congress, 133 separate bills were introduced to permit the transfer of trust land ownership from Indians to non-Indians.

With the Johnson administration in the 1960s the federal government began to reject termination. In the 1970s yet another Indian policy emerged. Known as "self-determination," it favored keeping the protective role of the federal government while increasing tribal participation in, and control of, important areas of local government. In 1983 President Reagan, in a policy statement on Indian affairs, restated the unique "government is government" relationship of the United States with the Indians. However, federal programs since then have moved toward transferring Indian affairs to individual states, which have long desired to gain control of Indian land and resources.

As long as American Indians retain power, land, and resources that are coveted by the states and the federal government, there will continue to be a "clash of cultures," and the issues will be contested in the courts, Congress, the White House, and even in the international human rights community. To give all Americans a greater comprehension of the issues and conflicts involving American Indians today is a major goal of this series. These issues are not easily understood, nor can these conflicts be readily resolved. The study of North American Indian history and culture is a necessary and important step toward that comprehension. All Americans must learn the history of the relations between the Indians and the federal government, recognize the unique legal status of the Indians, and understand the heritage and cultures of the Indians of North America.

Comanche Warrior, an engraving published in 1879.

STRANGERS
ON THE
PLAINS

For almost two centuries the Comanche helped shape the history of the American Southwest. They were a powerful group of people who fought fiercely and successfully to defend their land and way of life, so powerful that they were able to deal with many outsiders as superiors and with all others as equals.

For most of the 18th and 19th centuries the Comanche would dominate a vast region of the southern Plains. Indeed, the only Indians to threaten Comanche control seriously were the Apache, and they occupied the region for only a short time. The Comanche drove the Apache from the Plains and kept invaders, non-Indians and Indians alike, out of their land for almost 200 years. Their domination of most of what is now central and west Texas, eastern New Mexico, southeastern Colorado, southwestern Kansas, and all of western Oklahoma was so complete that until 1875 all of this land was known simply as the Comanchería, the land of the Comanche.

Foreign powers that entered the region had to contend with the Comanche as equals. In the 18th century both the French and Spanish sought their friendship. These Europeans were never able to occupy the region and penetrated it only with the grudging permission of the Comanche. The Mexicans and Texans who came afterward would also be unable to conquer the Comanche and settle on the southern Plains. In the 19th century both the Mexicans and Americans sought to establish and maintain good relations with them. The Comanchería would remain a barrier to settlement by outsiders until late in the 19th century, and the Americans would gain control of it only after a long and bloody struggle.

In the years before the Spanish came to North America the Comanche were mountain people, living in what are now the states of Wyoming and Montana. Little is now known of their history before 1705, when they were first mentioned by the Spanish. The Comanche had no written language and preserved their history only in the memories of their people. Much of their early history was lost when the people who remembered it died before it could be written down and saved. Not all was lost and forgotten, however. Even today the Comanche recall episodes from the very distant past. Other information about their lives long ago comes from

The dog and horse in this etching are both pulling travois, on which the Comanche carried their belongings when they moved camp to follow the buffalo herds. The Plains Indians used dogs for all their transportation needs until they acquired horses from the Spanish in the 17th century; after that they used both animals.

archaeologists and linguists. Archaeologists study artifacts excavated from sites dating back hundreds of years. Linguists analyze and compare languages. Combining Comanche oral traditions with evidence provided by these scholars and with the written records of the Europeans, we can piece together a general outline of their early history.

The Comanche still remember that long ago their ancestors were part of a larger group known as the Shoshone or the Snake people. They lived in the mountains of Wyoming and Montana north of the Arkansas River. They all spoke the same language, and archaeological evidence suggests that they lived in much the same way and hunted and camped in the same general area. They were a nomadic people, traveling to hunt, fish, and gather plant foods as different resources became available with the changing seasons. They traveled on foot, carrying their possessions on their backs or on the backs of their dogs.

The Shoshone's hunting and gathering way of life goes back many thousands of years. Indeed, it was this means of subsistence that the first Americans brought with them during the last Ice Age as they crossed the Bering land bridge between Asia and North America some 10,000 to 15,000 years ago. The Shoshone continued to live in this ancient way, as did their Comanche offshoot. There is no doubt that the Shoshone and the Comanche are related to one another and were at one time a single group of people. The Shoshone as well as the Comanche re-

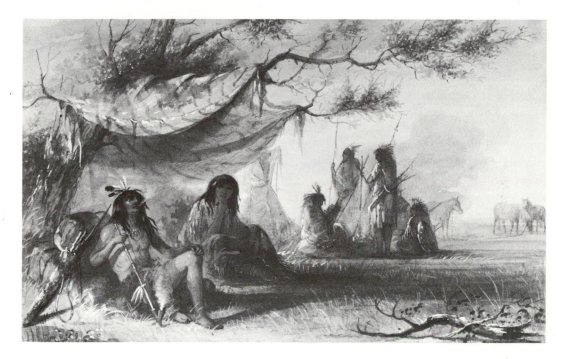

Eastern Shoshone encampment, painted by Alfred Jacob Miller from drawings made during a trip west in 1837. Until they moved onto the Plains in about 1700, the Comanche lived in the Wyoming and Montana mountains among their Shoshone kin.

call that the two groups were together a long time ago and acknowledge that they are related. The languages spoken today by the two peoples are very similar—so similar, in fact, that they can still understand each other. There are only a few minor differences in pronunciation and word order. Linguists consider all related languages to be members of a language family. The languages of the Shoshone and Comanche are members of the language family known as Uto-Aztecan, and both languages belong to the same branch of the Uto-Aztecan family, known as the Shoshone-Comanche-Koso division. Not only do these Indians speak the same language, but they share similar ideas about religion, family, society, and politics. These similarities confirm their joint history.

Additional confirmation comes from the sign language of the Plains Indians. There were many different peoples on the Great Plains, and they spoke a number of different languages. In order to communicate with one another, the Plains Indians developed a nonspoken language made up of hand gestures. The people who became the Comanche were referred to in the sign language of the Plains with a wiggling hand gesture that represented the movement of a snake. The Comanche never completely shed their mountain name and were sometimes called the Snake people in word and in sign.

Sometime around 1700 the Shoshone people became divided. Some bands abandoned the mountains and began moving south out onto the Plains. The Comanche still remember the division, and they have several stories that explain the separation.

One Comanche story relates that two bands of Shoshone were camped together. Boys from the two bands were playing together and during one of the games the son of one of the band leaders was kicked in the stomach by a boy from the other band. When the boy died from the injury his family wanted revenge and prepared to attack the other people. Before they began to fight, however, one of the old people convinced them that they should not fight with their own people. Both sides agreed that it was wrong to fight one's own people, but feelings were so intense that they decided they could no

Francisco Coronado in search of Quivera, a 1939 painting by N.C. Wyeth. Seeking a civilization he believed to be wealthy and powerful, Coronado entered the Plains in the spring of 1541. He was one of the first non-Indians to explore what would become Comanche territory.

longer stay together. Thus the two bands separated. One band went to the north, where they became the Shoshone. The other band went south and became known as the Comanche.

Another story about the separation also begins with two Shoshone bands camping and hunting together. During one of their combined hunts a bear was killed. Two hunters, one from each of the different bands, claimed to have shot the animal. Both bands claimed the bear carcass, and neither group was willing to share the meat. Both sides became angry. The dispute over the bear became so heated that the people decided that they could not stay together any longer. One group went north and the other group went south.

Still another account of the division of the Shoshone and the Comanche takes place in a large Shoshone camp. The people of the camp were attacked by some terrible disease, perhaps smallpox. The people were suffering and many were dying. They decided that they could not survive if they remained in one camp and that their only hope for survival was separation. One group went north and became the Shoshone and the other group went south and became known as the Comanche.

Perhaps there is some truth in all of these stories. The movement south did not take place all at once. It was a gradual movement of many Shoshone bands over a number of years. In the late 17th century some of the Shoshone began moving south and east into what is now Colorado. By 1700 several groups had abandoned the northern mountains and had begun living permanently on the southern Plains. They remained a nomadic hunting people, living in family bands, but they were no longer called the Shoshone. Those who moved to the Plains called themselves Nerm, Nimma, or Nermernuh, all of which translate as "People," or "Human Beings." The northern Shoshone bands continued to maintain friendly relations with their Comanche relatives well into the 20th century.

Meanwhile, Europeans were also moving into the region. The Spanish had arrived in the Southwest in the 16th century, having conquered Mexico in 1521. Lured into the region by tales of the Seven Cities of Gold, the conquistador Francisco Vásquez de Coronado explored the region in 1540. Finding no great wealth, Coronado returned to Mexico. In 1598, Don Juan de Oñate led another expedition north and established a Spanish settlement among the Indians in the Rio Grande valley. These people, who lived in villages made up of clusters of adobe buildings that the Spanish called pueblos, became known as the Pueblo Indians. They were farmers who irrigated their crops of corn, beans, squash, and cotton with water from nearby rivers and streams. When the Spanish arrived, there were more than 40,000 Pueblo Indians living in 66 separate and independent villages located along the northern Rio Grande and its tributaries.

The Spanish settled among the Pueblo people, establishing their own farms and ranches in the Rio Grande valley and using Indian land and water. They forced the Indians to work for them, to tend their fields and livestock. The Spanish also established missions among the Pueblos and worked diligently to destroy the Indians' religion and convert the Indians to their own faith, Roman Catholicism. When the Pueblo people resisted such treatment the Spanish crushed their resistance with force and brutality. The Indians tolerated the Spanish treatment for many years, but in August 1680, after 90 years of abuse and mistreatment, they rose up and attacked the newcomers. The Spanish, surprised and outnumbered, abandoned their homes and fled south so hastily that they had to leave most of their possessions behind. This uprising, known as the Pueblo Revolt, kept the Spanish out of the Southwest for 12 years, during which time the Pueblo people enjoyed freedom from Spanish demands.

The Indians had little use for most of the goods left behind by the Spanish. They did, however, enjoy one item the Spanish abandoned, the horse. The Spanish, intent on controlling the Indians, had attempted to keep horses from them. They knew that Indians riding horses would pose a threat to their control. Before the Pueblo Revolt the Spanish had refused to allow Indians to own or ride horses. Indians found with horses were beaten and sometimes killed. But the Pueblo people knew how to look after them: The Spanish had forced the Indians to feed and care for their horses. After the Spanish de-

parted, the Pueblos took the animals they left behind.

In 1692, Don Diego de Vargas led a Spanish army into what is now New Mexico and in a few years reconquered the region. The Spanish returned to the Rio Grande and reestablished their farms and missions. Once again they attempted to restrict the supply of horses, but they were unsuccessful, for it was difficult to lock up horses and prevent Indians from stealing them. Thus the region became and remained the most important source of horses for Indians throughout North America.

Horses permitted nomadic Indian people to enjoy a better life. Mounted Indian hunters could track their prey faster, cover greater distances in a day, and hunt more efficiently. They could take more game and provide their people with more food. When they traveled to follow the seasonal migration routes of their prey, they could move more quickly, and horses could carry their belongings. After Indians acquired horses, their lives became more comfortable. One group of Indians whose lives would be transformed by the use of the horse was the nomadic hunting people who arrived in the Southwest in the early 18th century. In 1705, just 13 years after the Reconquest began, Spanish officials wrote for the first time of a group of people called Comanche.

In southern Colorado some of the Plains Shoshone had traveled and hunted with another group of distantly related nomadic mountain hunting people, the Ute. The Ute had traded

The title page of a Spanish history of Texas written in the 1780s. The text reads "Memories for the history of the provinces of Texas written by the R.P.F. Juan Agustin de Morfi, retired reader and son of the province of the sacred gospel of Mexico."

meat, furs, and animal skins with the Spanish and Pueblo Indians for years before the Pueblo Revolt. The Pueblos gave them corn, beans, and other agricultural products. The Spanish, although unwilling to provide horses for the Ute, traded manufactured goods, largely metal items—knives, awls, hoes, pots and pans, and needles.

In the early 18th century the Ute, traveling with some of their Plains Shoshone kin, came to the Spanish settlements of New Mexico. It is from this meeting that these Shoshonean people received the name by which they are known today, the Comanche. They knew themselves as the Nerm, or Real People. We know them as the Comanche because the Spanish called them Komantcia. This is neither a Spanish word nor a Nerm word but the term used by the Ute for these people, Kwuma-ci or Koh-Mahts. This word has several possible meanings. It can mean "enemy" or "anyone who wants to fight us all the time." Most likely, however, it simply meant "stranger" in reference to the Nerm, who were not enemies of the Ute in 1705. The Spanish, able to communicate only with the Ute, used the Ute word and recorded it as Komantcia. The Ute also called the Cheyenne, Kiowa, and Arapaho Koh-Mahts, but it stuck only with the Nerm, and only they became known first to the Spanish, and later to the world, as Comanche.

The Comanche would not long remain strangers to the Spanish. More and more Comanche moved to the Plains and made it their home. No one is sure why these people continued to move south. Some believe they moved because the Crow and Dakota (Sioux) Indians in the north began pushing them south. Others believe that they were pulled south by their desire for Spanish horses and the immense buffalo herds of the southern Plains. Most likely a combination of both northern pressure and the attractiveness of the south convinced the Comanche to move onto the southern Plains. Here they would make their home. ▲

Buffalo Drinking and Bathing at Night, *painted by Alfred Jacob Miller from drawings he made in 1837. Buffalo herds on the Plains numbered in the millions, providing the Comanche and other Indians with almost everything they needed—food, fuel, clothing, shelter, tools, and more.*

2

COMANCHE
ON THE
SOUTHERN PLAINS

The southern Plains was a land with abundant food and a mild climate. The Comanche recognized the value of the land and began seizing it from the Apache. By the 1750s, they had forced the Apache out of the southern Plains. From the foothills of the mountains of New Mexico to the prairie forests of central Texas, known as the Cross Timbers, from the banks of the Arkansas River south to the Pecos River and the Rio Grande, the Comanche made this land their own.

The Comanchería was a vast land of more than 24,000 square miles, covered thickly with rich grass. Although the land was generally level, it was broken in places by deep valleys, isolated, steep hills rising abruptly out of the flat country, and long, raised earthen ridges and cliff faces known as escarpments. In the north lay the Wichita Mountains, an island of rugged hills in the sea of grass. To the west there was an enormous raised stretch of flat land known as the Llano Estacado, or Staked Plain. The Comanchería stretched southward to the edges of the Edwards Plateau, and east through the rolling hills of the prairie to Cross Timbers.

This dry, flat land was crossed by several large rivers that flowed from the northwest across to the southeast—the Cimarron, Canadian, Washita, Red, Pease, Brazos, and Pecos. All were wide and shallow, often more than 100 yards wide, seldom more than 2 or 3 feet deep. As they cut across the Comanchería, draining the high land of the northwest, the rivers picked up gypsum and other minerals and became unsuitable for drinking. There were few trees, and only along these wide meandering rivers could brush thickets and stands of trees grow. Although the land was largely timberless and the rivers brackish, the Comanchería had abundant natural resources. The thick, rich grass supported the millions of buffalo, elk, deer, and antelope that roamed throughout the region. The rivers, fed by clear streams and springs, were sparsely lined with cottonwood, elm, walnut, pecan, and persimmon trees that provided food and shelter for the Comanche.

The weather was relatively mild. The summers were hot and dry, but the Comanche always knew where to find fresh water. They knew how to construct tipis so that fresh air could circulate inside and how to build arbors to provide shelter from the glaring, hot sun. The winters were cold, but less bitter than the winters the Comanche had known in the mountains of Colorado and Wyoming. In the winter the Comanche set up their camps in the shelter of the canyons and the breaks of the escarpments, where they escaped the full force of the Plains blizzards that came down from the north.

The Comanche brought their Shoshone mountain way of life with them when they moved to the southern Plains. As mountain people they had

A camp of the Quahadi band of Comanche, photographed in the 1860s. In summer the tipi covering was folded up so air could enter the interior.

been organized in extended family hunting groups, and they moved to the Plains in these same small groups. Family groups would often join together to form an autonomous and independent band. Such bands varied in size and could consist of a single family hunting group or as many as several hundred people. These bands were loosely organized and not restricted to blood relatives. Any Comanche was free to leave one band and join another. All were Comanche.

The Comanche's social and political organizations were those of a hunting people, well suited for life on the southern Plains. They shared a common language and way of life. They knew that they were all one people, even though they had no overall tribal organization. Several bands living in the same general area might occasionally come together to form a larger grouping to hunt or raid. In time all the local bands living in one general area acquired a name and came to have a distinctive identity. These divisions were distinguished by various regional characteristics. The division operating in one area might speak more slowly than one from another area. One group of bands might prefer antelope-skin clothing, whereas those in another region might use only deerskin. The differences between regional divisions were seldom significant, and all Comanche felt free to live among the various divisions.

It is not clear just how many divisions existed nor how long they survived. The Spanish and Americans recorded the names of at least 13 identifiable regional divisions in the 18th and 19th centuries. Some existed only in the 18th century, and some only in the 19th. Some Comanche bands merged to form larger divisions. Some bands survived whereas others divided and reformed to create new ones. Some bands became extinct, and some still exist today.

For much of their history the Comanche consisted of five major regional divisions, each of which was made up of several local bands. One of the largest divisions was the Penateka, whose name means Honey-Eaters. These Indians occupied the southernmost portion of the Comanchería, along the edge of the Edwards Plateau across to the Cross Timbers. They lived near the Spanish settlements in Texas and were known to the Spanish as the Southern Comanche. They were also known as the Penane (Wasps) and the Hois (Timber People) because they lived in the only portion of the Comanchería where there were many trees, in which they found the wild honey that gave them their name. Although they were called the Honey-Eaters, the Penateka, like other Comanche, relied primarily on the buffalo for food.

North of the Penateka, in the eastern part of the Comanchería in the region between the Colorado and Red rivers, were the Nokoni Comanche. Nokoni means "Those Who Turn Back" or "Wanderers." This division took its name from one of its leaders. After he died the people were uneasy at using the name of a dead person. They took a new name and were known thereafter as the Detsanayuka, or "Wanderers Who Never Set Up Good Camps." Perhaps this name referred to their extremely nomadic way of life, for they apparently moved more frequently than other Comanche divisions and never took the time to establish proper camps. Two other smaller Comanche divisions lived just south of the Nokoni. They were the Tenawa, "Those Who Stay Downstream," and the Tanima, "Liver Eaters." Together the Nokoni, Tenawa, and Tanima were known as the Middle Comanche.

In the Red River valley, just north of the Nokoni between the Red River and the Canadian River, lived the seven or eight bands that made up the Kotsoteka, or "Buffalo Eaters." All Comanche ate buffalo meat, of course, and all relied on the buffalo for most of their diet and other needs, but this division lived in a region where particularly great herds of buffalo could always be found. Just north of the Kotsoteka were the northernmost Comanche, the Yamparika, whose name means "Yampa (Root) Eaters." This division consisted of the last band to leave the mountains, and although they also relied primarily on the buffalo for food, they still retained the old Shoshone custom of digging and eating the thick edible roots of the Yampa vine. The Yamparika never forgot their Shoshone kin and remained friendly with them.

A sixth Comanche division that became particularly important in the 19th century was the western Comanche or the Quahadi (Antelope). The Quahadi bands may not have formed until the 19th century. This group seems to have consisted primarily of Kotsoteka Comanche who moved south from the Cimarron Valley to the isolation of the high plains of the Llano Estacado.

These five divisions—the Penateka, Nokoni and the other middle Comanche, Kotsoteka, Yamparika, and Quahadi—were the major historic Comanche groups. Each consisted of several local bands that lived in the same general area and shared minor cultural characteristics. There were also other named Comanche groups that we know little about—the Iteta-o (Burnt Meat), the Mutsane or Mot-sai (Undercut Bank), the Pahuraix (Water Horse), Wia'ne (Hill Wearing Away), the It-chit-a bud-ah (Cold People), and the Haine-an-une (Corn Eaters). These groupings may have been small bands within the larger regional divisions. All were short lived and were no longer distinct by the 19th century.

The size and membership of the divisions varied. Altogether there may have been about 20,000 Comanche living in the 5 major divisions. A regional division may have contained as many as 5,000 people living in the same general area. Some of the bands may have been larger and others, particularly the Quahadi, were probably smaller. Even within the larger regional divisions the bands operated without much regard for neighboring divisions. Indeed, the Penateka, the southernmost of the Co-

COMANCHE BAND LOCATIONS ON THE COMANCHERÍA 1750–1840

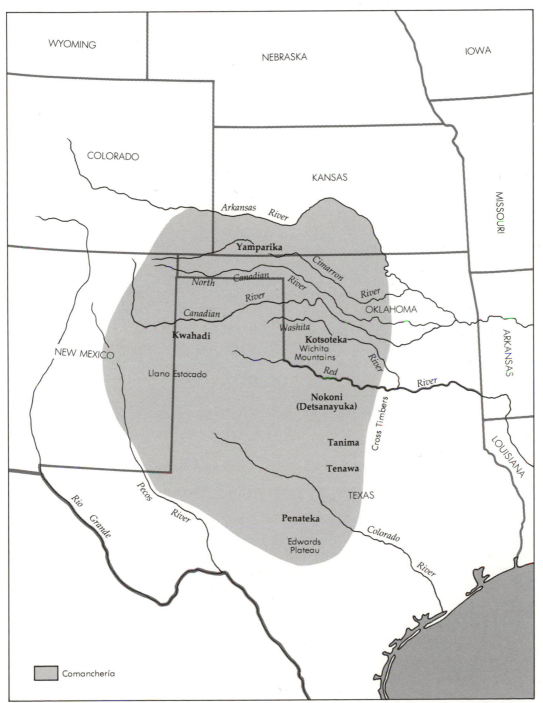

Comanche chief Ee-shah-ko-nee (Bow and Quiver), sketched by George Catlin in 1834. The artist wrote, "The head chief of this village . . . dressed in a very humble manner. . . . [His only ornaments are] a couple of beautiful shells worn in his ears, and a boar's tusk attacked to his neck."

manche, lived almost 500 miles to the south and seldom had any contact with the northern bands of the Kotsoteka and Yamparika. No one leader spoke for all of the Penateka or Yamparika. Each band was independent, each regional division was autonomous, and no overall tribal organization existed. All, however, were Comanche. Although they never fought together as a single unit, they never fought one another. This loose and limited unity cre-

ated by a common cultural identity gave them great strength against outsiders.

The Comanche had few political institutions. There was no overall tribal government and no tribal leader or tribal council able to speak for or direct the activities of all the Comanche. There were only three sources of political power—peace chief, band council, and war chief—and the powers of each were severely limited. None of the three had much direct authority.

Within the band, each family group had a leader called the peace chief, usually one of the oldest men in the group. The peace chiefs were thought of as fathers of the band, but their powers were limited. They could only advise and suggest. When several family groups came together one of the peace chiefs was usually recognized as peace chief or leader for the combined group. He served in this capacity only as long as the bands stayed together. The other band peace chiefs acted as advisers to the group leader.

A man became a peace chief not by election but by general consent. The Comanche respected the elderly, and one who was wise, talented, generous, and kind might in time become his family's peace chief. His leadership depended on the respect the people had for him, his popularity, and his influence. He could not force the people to do anything; his primary responsibility was to act as a mediator to keep peace within the band. To do this he relied on persuasion. His influence was limited to the internal affairs of his band and did not extend beyond his band. He held his position for only as long as the people listened to him and followed his advice. Although the office was not inherited, the sons of peace chiefs frequently replaced their fathers as band leaders. A father's training, experience, and example prepared his sons to assume leadership when he died. However, the position was open to any skillful Comanche man who was consistently even tempered and who displayed the valued leadership qualities of good sense, wisdom, and generosity.

Important decisions were made by the band council, which consisted of all the adult men in the band. All men were allowed to speak in the council meetings, but the older men did most of the talking. Women did not normally participate but could listen to the council meeting and speak before the council if called upon by the men. The council decided when and where the band should move and provided for the care of elderly and weak band members. It made decisions about war and peace, established alliances with other bands, and made decisions about trade with outsiders.

The Comanche believed that important decisions must be unanimous. During the council meetings, all could speak and present their views. When all the men agreed and a consensus was reached, the decision was announced to the people by criers. It was not always possible to achieve general agreement, but the Comanche believed that they needed unanimity in order to preserve harmony and unity within the band. If they could not all agree the council postponed the decision. A person who could not accept a council's decision would always leave the band. If enough people felt the same way, they might break away and form a new group with new leadership. Such a split might have been the cause of the Comanche leaving their Shoshone kin in the mountains and moving to the Plains around 1700. Because of the need for consensus, a council sometimes followed rather than led popular opinion.

This was particularly likely to be true in time of warfare. Civil leadership was separated from military leadership. Individuals who distinguished themselves in battle were admired and respected. Band councils recognized the most successful and respected warrior and chose him to be war chief for the band. The council based its decision on the individual's military exploits and the opinions of the other warriors.

During a war expedition the war leader was in charge. He directed the group and gave orders to the men, who had to obey him or leave the group. But even during a war expedition there were limits to the war chief's powers. Because people joined the groups voluntarily, they always had the right to leave at any time. The war leader's authority to tell people what to do lasted only as long as the raid. After the group returned to the band he lost his power to tell others what to do.

Although the Comanche bands recognized their outstanding warriors as

Comanche men, sketched by George Catlin in 1834. Catlin was traveling with an expedition whose aim was "to see the chiefs of the Camanchees . . . to shake hands with them, and to smoke the pipe of peace, and to establish an acquaintance, and consequently a system of trade that would be beneficial to both."

the band war chiefs, any Comanche could lead a war party on a raid. A warrior who wanted to lead a raid could simply announce his plans to do so; if he had a reputation for bravery and success others might follow him. The band council did not have to authorize the raid. A warrior who had continued success and showed generosity by sharing the goods gathered on raids would gain respect, status, and greater influence within the group.

The war leader was the only Comanche who had the authority to direct others' behavior, and even he possessed that power for only a short time. The peace chief held power for a long time but also had only limited powers. The band council had only limited authority because it could make no decisions until or unless all the members of the band agreed. Individuals always had the right to leave the band and ignore the decisions of the council or peace chief, or the orders of a war leader.

Each Comanche band operated independently. Sometimes a few bands camped together and sometimes band peace chiefs met with the peace chiefs and councils of other bands. Bands sometimes raided together but more often they remained apart. This lack of a unified tribal organization worked well for the Comanche. They remained linked by language and culture while living in scattered, mobile communities stretched out over the 24,000 square miles of the Comanchería. Traveling in small bands, hunting the abundant game of their new homeland, the Comanche prospered. Buffalo, deer, elk, and antelope were so plentiful on the southern Plains that the Comanche could easily hunt all they needed without coming together for great communal hunts in the summer as most other Plains Indian peoples did. The Comanche had left the northern mountains in bands, and although they became Plains people they retained much of their mountain hunting culture. ▲

Buffalo Hunt, *painted by Alfred Jacob Miller, who traveled to the West in 1837. One method of hunting was to stampede the buffalo and drive them over a cliff. The Comanche could easily pick off those that were wounded after the herd thundered past.*

3

LIFE
ON THE
COMANCHERÍA

Before moving onto the Plains the Comanche had been a nomadic people who hunted and traveled on foot. When their game moved, the Comanche were forced to follow them. They packed up their possessions and moved on. The buffalo and the horse were central to their life. The Comanche skillfully used the natural products of the Comanchería, but they never planted or cultivated any crops. They remained a nomadic hunting people. After moving to the southern Plains, they continued to follow this way of life.

Having horses reinforced the cultural patterns that already existed. The horse transformed the Comanche from nomadic foot hunters living close to the edge of survival into a healthy and prosperous people. Taking advantage of the mobility and speed of the horses, the Comanche became skillful and efficient buffalo hunters. They could travel

greater distances, find buffalo more easily, and bring down more game. They could carry the game farther and save more of it. Mounted Comanche hunters could always provide their people with enough food, clothing, and shelter. No longer did the Comanche have to trail after animals on foot, hoping for lucky hunting, nor did they have to go hungry when the game abandoned the region.

With the horse and the buffalo the Comanche thrived. Now the old, young, ill, and weak were all well nourished and so could survive better. The Comanche population grew in the 18th century. It is not possible to know exactly how many Comanche were in the bands that came down from the mountains, nor how many there were in the 18th and 19th centuries before they were counted in U.S. government censuses. Historical accounts, however, provide some clues that allow scholars to estimate the Plains Comanche population. Often the documents describe how many villages there were, the number of lodges or warriors in a camp, or how many people lived in one lodge. From these few numbers it has been estimated that by the mid-18th century there were at least 20,000 Comanche living on the southern Plains. Epidemics of smallpox and other diseases in the 1830s and 1840s caused a significant decline in the Comanche population. Other deprivations in the last half of the century would cause the population to drop dramatically, until by 1899 there were about 2,000 Comanche.

Not only did horses contribute to better hunting and a better life, but they thrived on the Comanchería grass. In the winter, when the grass lay dormant, the horses could subsist on bark from the cottonwood trees that grew along the rivers and streams. When times were especially bleak the Comanche could and did eat their horses. Horses were also useful trade items. Other Indians as well as Europeans and non-Indian Americans living far from the Spanish Southwest desired horses, and the Comanche became talented horse traders, getting tobacco, woven cloth, and especially metal items, such as knives, in return.

The Comanche became superb riders. Several 19th-century observers maintained that they were the finest horsemen in all of North America. Comanche children began riding at an early age, and all Comanche, men and women alike, spent much of their lives on the back of a horse. The Comanche were skillful horse breeders, and they also excelled at capturing wild horses. There were many herds of wild horses in the Comanchería, and Comanche often chased them down in the open country and roped them with lassos. They made ropes for lassos from material they had at hand: They cut long strips of buffalo hide into strong ropes, braided buffalo wool, and twisted and braided hair from the manes and tails of horses.

To capture wild horses and manage their herds, the Comanche constructed large pens or corrals near water holes out on the plains. They used trees and brush to form the fencelike walls of the corrals, which were oval and open only at one end. Extending out from both sides of the corral opening they stacked long piles of brush thick and high enough so that the horses could not run through or jump over them. These brush arms of the corral extended for hundreds of yards, the space between them widening as they opened toward the plains to form a fan-shaped passageway. The Comanche would surround a herd of wild horses and drive them into the wide, open end of the passageway. As the horses got closer to the corral the passageway became narrower, funneling the horses into the corral where the Comanche could more easily rope them. The Indians would often wait near a water hole until wild horses arrived and drank their fill. They then rushed among them and readily

Buffalo Rift, *a painting by Alfred Jacob Miller. Comanches captured wild horses by lassoing them out of a herd.*

captured the slower, water-logged animals. The Comanche also hunted wild horses in the winter, when the animals, weakened by cold weather and lack of food, were slower and easier to capture.

A particularly popular way of acquiring horses was to steal them from others. The Comanche were talented horse thieves. In their value system, stealing from strangers was acceptable behavior. Like other Indian peoples, they established friendships with outsiders and maintained these friendships by exchanging gifts and sharing. In this way they maintained long-term friendly relations with Indian and Spanish traders. But any outsiders with whom they had not established a friendship were fair game. One shared with one's family and friends and stole from strangers. The Comanche raided and stole from their Spanish and Pueblo Indian neighbors in New Mexico and the Spanish settlements in Texas and northern Mexico. They would attack entire communities and drive the horses away with them; individual Comanches also often slipped undetected into the camps of enemies and stole their horses. Colonel Henry Dodge, an American soldier who fought the Comanche in the 19th century, claimed that a Comanche could slip into a camp "where a dozen men were sleeping, each with a horse tied to his wrist by the lariat [lasso], and a rope within six feet of the sleeper and get away with the horse without waking a soul."

The Comanche kept large herds: It was not unusual for a single Comanche to own more than 250 horses, and a particularly prominent leader might own as many as 1,000. Keeping such large herds contributed to Comanche movement. They had to keep moving their camps, not only to find the buffalo but also to find grass to feed their thousands of horses.

The buffalo provided food, clothing, shelter, and tools for the Indians. Buffalo ranged all over North America but were most concentrated on the Great Plains. There is no way to know exactly how many buffalo there were in North America in the past, but scholars estimate that there were more than 60 million buffalo when the Europeans first arrived in the early 16th century. The

Comanche Village, Women Dressing Robes and Drying Meat, *painted by George Catlin in 1834. Women were responsible for processing and preparing hides, making clothing, storing supplies for winter months, and putting up and taking down the family tipis.*

great herds migrated with the seasons, but a large portion of the southern herd always remained south of the Arkansas River. Because of the animals' continual presence on the southern Plains, the Comanche always had an ample supply of buffalo.

Indian people had hunted buffalo since long before they acquired horses. Hunting on foot, Indian people used fire and stampedes to drive the buffalo off steep cliffs. Much of a herd would be killed, either from the fall itself, from being trampled by other animals, or from the arrows and lances of the hunters. When the Indians killed more animals than they could butcher, much meat and hide were wasted. After the Comanche got horses, they did not have to rely on the inefficient mass slaughter of buffalo that occurred when they had to drive entire herds off cliffs. Comanche hunters, mounted on Spanish horses, became superb buffalo hunters.

There were plenty of buffalo in the region at every season so the Comanche could hunt them year-round. The best time to hunt, however, was in the late fall. As winter approached the buffalo put on extra fat and grew thicker pelts. Sometime in November the Comanche would leave their camps along the river valleys and move out onto the Plains to hunt the winter buffalo. The Indians usually remained out on the Plains until snow and cold weather drove them back to the sheltered regions of the hills to the North.

Because small hunting parties could easily succeed among the great herds on the southern Plains, the Comanche had no need for large, coordinated hunts. They seldom had to maintain much control over their hunters. Sometimes they selected a hunt leader who would decide as they approached a herd when and where they would camp and hunt. After they sighted the buffalo, however, the Comanche hunted individually, without direction from the hunt leader. This was quite unlike the practice of most Plains Indian peoples: On the northern Plains, where there were more people and fewer buffalo, buffalo hunts were tightly controlled by hunt leaders and closely supervised by warriors acting as hunt police.

The Comanche hunted with bows and arrows. Although some Comanche used bows made from the horns of buffalo and elk, most used wooden bows. Old Comanche men who could no longer hunt or go to war made most of the bows. It took great skill and months of preparation to make a good bow. The Comanche used various kinds of wood, but the wood from the Osage orange tree, also known as *bois d'arc*, or "wood for the bow," was the most popular. This tree, common along the river bottoms of the Comanchería, had wood that was strong, flexible, and durable. Wood for bows was cut from a still-green tree into four-foot lengths and scraped and shaved down into thin three-foot lengths. Before any further work was done on the wood, it was

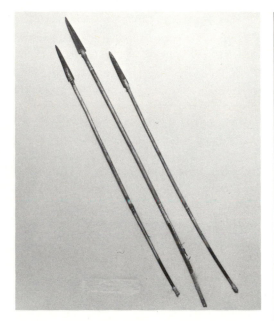

Comanche arrows with metal tips attached to the wooden shafts. The tips on the two outer arrows were carefully hammered and shaped to fit snugly around the shaft, making the tip more secure and therefore less likely to be lost when the arrow was shot.

allowed to dry. Drying might take several months, depending on the weather and the moisture in the wood. Once dry, the bow was whittled down to its final shape and greased with animal fat to make it more flexible and water-resistant. The bow wood was then tightly wrapped with thin wet strips of buffalo sinew (tendon). The sinew was covered with glue made by boiling animal horns and hooves in water for hours. After the glue dried and hardened, the sinew shrank to form a tight covering over the bow wood. Next the bowstring had to be prepared. Bowstrings, too, were made by specialists, again usually older

Comanche men. They shredded buffalo sinew into long fibrous strips and soaked the fibers in glue thinned with water. Then, while the fibers were still wet with glue, the men twisted them into a long, single string. When the glue dried, the string would be strong and pliable. The string was then tied and glued to the bow. Finally, the bow was ready for use.

Often the same old men who made the bows and bowstrings were the specialists who made the arrows. Arrows had to be the proper length and weight in order to fly straight and true. Arrow-makers cut wood from dogwood and mulberry trees and shaped it into thin strips. The wood was then allowed to dry and, once dry, the arrows were scraped and carved down to the proper weight and size. Feathers, usually from wild turkeys or owls, were glued to one end and arrowheads were tied and glued to the other. Flint, which was easily worked, was the most popular material for arrowheads, but points were made from other types of stone and sometimes from sharpened pieces of bone and horn. After the Comanche began trading with the Europeans in the 18th century, they began using metal for arrowheads. They cut, hammered, and filed down pieces of metal and fastened them to the arrows with glue and sinew.

Using their short wooden bows, the Comanche could drive an arrow through a buffalo at close range. Mounted on their best-trained hunting horses, Comanche hunters would charge in among the buffalo. Each hunter would choose one and ride up from behind it. As he came alongside the beast he shot an arrow into its body between the hip and rib cage. Although most Comanche hunters used only a bow and arrows, some used a long wooden lance to spear the buffalo. They would ride alongside the buffalo and plunge the 14-foot lance into the great animal's side. The bow and arrow and the lance were such excellent weapons for hunting that the Comanche continued to rely solely on them even after they acquired guns. Muskets firing black powder were ill suited for buffalo hunting. The muskets had great range but were awkward to load and aim while on the back of a racing horse. Comanche warriors became skilled in loading and shooting their guns while on horseback, but they could shoot more arrows in less time than it took to fire and reload a gun. Moreover, they could not always get guns and ammunition from the traders, but they had an inexhaustible supply of the bows and arrows that they made themselves.

The buffalo provided ample food for the people as well as raw materials for their other needs. The Comanche used almost all of the animal and wasted little. They ate the fresh meat and cut and dried the surplus meat for later use. They used the stomach and intestines for water bags and boiled meat in the paunches. They scraped out and cleaned the buffalo horns and used them for bowls, cups, and spoons. They made scrapers and other tools from bones, some of which they split into sharp splinters for use as needles or awls. They tanned buffalo hides, making warm robes and blankets from the thick winter pelts, clothing and tipi covers from scraped hides. They fashioned containers and various other objects from untanned hides.

Comanche women prepared buffalo hides for robes, tipi covers, and other uses. They skinned the buffalo and stretched the hides on wooden racks or staked them out on the ground. Using bone or metal scrapers they scraped the underside of the hide until all the flesh was removed. When making tent covers they scraped both sides of the skin to remove the buffalo wool as well as the flesh. When the hide was clean, the women rubbed a mixture of animal brains, livers, tree bark, grease, and water into it to tan and preserve it. They rubbed this tanning mixture into the hide for hours, then pulled and stretched the hide to make it soft and flexible. This process was repeated day after day until the skin was soft.

Although they relied primarily on the buffalo, the Comanche also hunted other animals of the Comanchería. They hunted elk, deer, and antelope and also used their meat for food, their hides for clothing, and the bones for tools.

The way of life the Comanche created was suited to their nomadic food-getting requirements. They lived in bands that camped alongside a source of fresh water. Larger camps might stretch for miles along a stream or river. Within the camps, Comanche might set up their homes near those of their close relatives, but unlike other Plains Indian

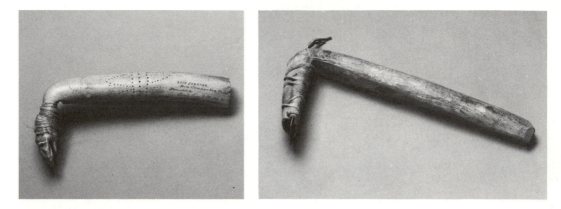

Bone-handled scrapers for preparing hides. The one at left has a stone blade; the one at right, a metal blade. Stone cutting edges wore down quickly and tended to fracture and break often. For this reason, the Indians quickly became dependent on metal European trade items.

peoples, they did not arrange their tipis in any special order.

The Comanche lived in buffalo-skin tipis. This conical tent was practical and portable. A Comanche woman could set one up or take one down in about 15 minutes. Each tipi was made up of a framework of long slender wooden poles with a buffalo-skin cover. The poles, usually made of pine or cedar, were from 12 to 20 feet long. The Comanche tipi was erected on a four-pole foundation. Comanche women tied four poles together near one end and raised them up, setting the other ends firmly into the earth. The long ends extended out from the top. About 18 other poles were placed between the foundation poles and tied to them at the top. The ends of these poles, too, were inserted into the ground. The base of the tipi formed a circle 12 to 15 feet in diameter. A covering of buffalo skin, tanned and with the wool removed, was stretched tightly over and attached

to the wooden framework. To make the tipi cover, a woman sewed from 10 to 17 hides together, the number depending on the size of the skins. Tipis were usually 12 to 14 feet high. Comanche men sometimes decorated the outside of their tipi by painting abstract designs and geometric figures on the tipi cover.

The hide cover was left open near the top of the tipi, just below where the lodge poles were tied together, to create a smoke hole. The size of the opening could be adjusted by folding or unfolding flaps of the tipi cover. The doorway was a small opening near the base of the tipi, directly below the smoke flap; it was covered by a stiff piece of tanned leather or a large flap of bearskin.

The tipi cover was held in place by stakes driven through the base and into the earth. In warm weather the women would not draw the cover all the way down to the ground when they set up their tipis but would leave a gap along the bottom to allow fresh air to enter and cool the interior. This provided excellent ventilation and created a draft that carried smoke from the tipi fire up and out of the smoke hole. Usually the Comanche hung a skin liner inside the lower part of the tipi. The liner was hung from the poles and the ends were tucked under the edges of the bed platforms around the inside. This liner protected the Comanche from the strong winds of the Comanchería, yet permitted fresh air to enter under the outside walls.

Inside, the tipis were simply furnished. Directly opposite the entrance, against the back wall, was the bed of the owner of the tipi. The beds of other family members were around the base. Beds consisted of a soft pile of buffalo robes. Sometimes the robes were heaped on a low platform, constructed by stretching broad strips of rawhide across a wooden framework. These platforms raised the beds off the cold ground. The Comanche stored their clothing, food, and any personal items in large pouches made of untanned buffalo hide. These leather pouches, called parfleches (rawhides) by the Europeans, were kept under the beds, leaned against the walls, and hung from the lodge poles. Parfleches were easy to make, pack, and carry.

A small fire was kept burning in the center of the tipi. When the weather was extremely cold food was cooked inside the lodge, but otherwise cooking was done on larger fires outside. During the hot southern Plains summers the Comanche often slept outside. They would erect a brush shelter, a simple flat-roofed arbor made of a wooden framework that was covered with leafy branches. The sides were left open. Here the Comanche could escape the sun and heat of the day and enjoy the cool breezes at night. The tipi was ideal for the Comanche's nomadic way of life. Constructed from natural products abundant in the region, it was sturdy and portable. It was warm in the winter and cool in the summer. Europeans and, later, Americans would observe that the tipi was warmer and more comfortable than the dugout sod houses and cabins used by the first non-Indians to settle on the southern Plains. It was an excellent shelter for a hunting people who lived their life on the move.

Comanche clothing was practical and, like the tipis, made from natural materials of the Comanchería. Young boys seldom wore any clothing at all, unless the weather was cold. When

This Spanish painting depicts a Comanche family in traditional clothing. The man wears a buffalo-skin robe and a breechclout, the woman, a buckskin shirt and skirt; the baby is on a cradle board wrapped in buckskin.

they reached the age of eight or nine, they began wearing the clothing of an adult Comanche. Men wore a leather belt with a breechclout. The breechclout was a long piece of buckskin that they brought up between their legs and looped over and under their belt in front and back. They wore close-fitting deerskin leggings to cover their legs. The leggings were tied to their belt and extended down to their moccasins. The moccasins had soles made from thick, tough buffalo hide with soft deerskin uppers. The Comanche usually wore nothing on their upper body, but in winter they wore heavy, warm buffalo robes around their shoulders and knee-

These Comanche woman's moccasins with attached leggings are made of tanned buckskin dyed yellow and decorated with fringe, beads, and German silver buttons. The soles are of rawhide.

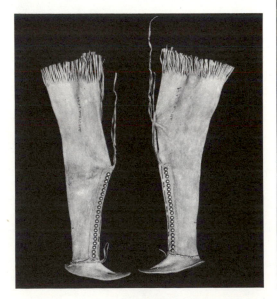

length buffalo-hide winter boots. They sometimes wore robes made of bear, wolf, or coyote skins. In the 19th century woven cloth replaced the buckskin breechclouts, and the men began wearing loose-fitting buckskin shirts. They decorated their shirts, leggings, and moccasins with fringe made of deerskin, animal fur, and human hair. They also decorated their shirts and leggings with patterns and shapes formed with beads and bits of metal. Comanche men also wore bands of leather and strips of metal on their arms.

Comanche women's clothing was also made from deerskin. Unlike the boys, young girls did not go naked. As soon as they could walk they wore a belt and breechclout. By about 12 or 13 years of age they began wearing the clothing of an adult Comanche woman. Comanche women wore a long one-piece dress made of buckskin. The dress had a flared skirt and wide, long sleeves and was trimmed with buckskin fringe along the sleeves and hem. Beads and bits of metal were attached in geometric patterns. Comanche women wore buckskin moccasins with buffalo-hide soles. In the winter they, too, wore warm buffalo robes and tall, fur-lined buffalo-hide boots.

Comanche men took great pride in their hair, which they seldom cut, allowing it to grow very long. They arranged their hair with porcupine quill brushes, greased it, and parted it in the center from the forehead to the back of the neck. They painted the scalp along the part with yellow, red, or white clay

Buffalo-scalp war headdress, a type worn by some Comanche warriors.

or other colors and wore their hair in two long braids. They tied their braids with leather thongs or colored cloth and sometimes wrapped the braids with beaver fur. They also braided a strand of hair from the top of their head. This slender braid dangling from their head was called a scalp lock and was decorated with colored bits of cloth, beads, and a single feather. The feather had no special meaning for the Comanche and was worn solely for decoration. They had no tradition of wearing the large feathered bonnets seen among the northern Plains peoples. Only after they moved onto a reservation late in the 19th century would Comanche men adopt the typical Plains headdress.

Comanche men rarely wore anything on their heads. If the winter was severely cold they might wear a brimless, woolly buffalo hide hat. When they went to war some warriors wore a headdress made from the scalp of a buffalo's head. Comanche warriors cut away most of the hide from a buffalo head and scraped away most of the flesh, leaving only a portion of the woolly hair and the horns. This woolly, horned buffalo hat was only worn when raiding and was only worn by the Comanche.

Comanche women did not let their hair grow as long as the men did. Young girls might wear their hair long and braided, but women parted their hair in the middle and kept it short. Like the men, they painted their scalp along their part with bright paint.

Comanche men usually had pierced ears from which hung earrings of bits of shell or loops of brass or silver wire. A female relative would pierce the outer edge of each ear with six or eight holes. Comanche men also tattooed their face, arms, and chest with geometric designs and painted their face and body. Originally they had used paints made from berry juice and the colored clays of the Comanchería. Later, traders supplied

Comanche feats of Horsemanship—Sham Battle, *painted by George Catlin in 1835. The artist wrote that "among their feats of riding [one] astonished me. . . . Every young man . . . is able to drop his body upon the side of his horse . . . effectually screened from his enemies' weapons as he lays in a horizontal position . . . with his heel hanging over the horse's back; by which he has the power of throwing himself up again, and changing to the other side of the horse if necessary. . . . He will hang whilst his horse is at fullest speed, carrying with him his bow and his shield, and also his long lance."*

them with vermilion (red pigment) and bright grease paints. There was no standard pattern for face and body painting among the Comanche and, with the exception of black paint, which was the color for war, there was no particular significance attached to specific colors. Design and color were up to the individual and might have special meaning for some people. Special colors and designs might have been revealed to them in a dream. One Comanche might always paint himself in a particular way, whereas others might change their designs and colors whenever they felt like it. One might paint one side of his face white and the other side red. Another might paint an entire side of his body green while the other side would be yellow with black stripes.

Comanche women might also tattoo their face, arms, and breasts. They were fond of body painting and were also free to paint themselves however they pleased. A popular pattern among Comanche women was to paint the insides of their ears a bright red and paint great orange and red circles on their cheeks. They usually painted red and yellow lines around their eyes.

The Comanche way of life changed on the Plains, but true to their cultural heritage they remained a nomadic hunting people. They struck compromises with their new environment to create a way of life that combined the old with the new. They differed from other Plains tribes in numerous ways. Unlike the Plains people living north of them, the Comanche never came together for great communal summer hunts or other reasons. Only a few bands came together at the time of the November winter hunt. Indeed, the Comanche bands never had close contact with one another until they were confined on a small reservation in Indian Territory after 1875. All other Plains tribes practiced a ceremony known as the Sun Dance when they gathered together in great summer encampments. The Sun Dance required much energy and sacrifice, but Plains people believed that if it was conducted properly the Great Spirit would bless the people and give them great strength and a continuing supply of buffalo and other food. Only once, in 1874, when they faced hard times, did the Comanche conduct a Sun Dance, assisted by their friends to the north, the Kiowa, a Plains tribe that used the Sun Dance regularly. Only a few Comanche bands participated. The Comanche never held a Sun Dance again.

The Comanche were also unique among the Plains Indians in having no separate soldiers' societies. Comanche men were as brave as those of the Cheyenne or the Dakota Sioux, but they had no military societies. Nevertheless, they conquered the Comanchería and kept others out of their territory for more than a century and a half. ▲

Comanche warriors returning from a horse-stealing raid, painted by Charles M. Russell in 1911.

CONQUEST
OF THE
SOUTHERN PLAINS

After the Comanche moved to the southern Plains in the early 18th century, they engaged in a fierce struggle to take and then keep their land. Although not at war for all of the next 175 years, they spent much of the time in conflict with the nations that surrounded them. The Comanche went to war not simply for individual glory, loot, and revenge, but for very real political and economic reasons as well.

Their invasion of the southern Plains was pushed by larger and better-armed tribes in the north and pulled by the buffalo and horses to the south. On the Plains they came into conflict with the Apache people who were living there. The life-and-death struggle with the Apache for the precious resources of the southern Plains was a bitter battle with a critical outcome. The Comanche fought to acquire the buffalo and horses of the region, and the Apache fought to keep them.

After driving the Apache from the heart of the region, the Comanche continued fighting, for they were surrounded by other Indian groups that coveted their horses, their women, their children, and their land. Apaches remained in the west and the south. The Pawnee, Cheyenne, Arapaho, and Kiowa to the north were early threats. The Osage living to the northeast challenged the Comanche, as did the Wichita, Taovayas, Tawakoni, and other Caddoan-speaking people living along the Red River. Still other Caddoan groups—the Hasinai, Anadarko, Nabedache, and Nacono on the east as well as the Tonkawa to the south and east—would continue to threaten them. Mounted on Spanish horses, Comanches raided south deep into Mexico. They raided Spanish and Pueblo Indian communities in New Mexico and Spanish outposts and the Apache in Texas. They fought the Pawnee and the Osage for the buffalo country along the Arkansas River. Throughout the 18th and 19th centuries the Comanche were constantly in competition with others. They did not fight all of their neighbors at all times, and not all Comanche bands fought against the same groups. At times some bands might make peace with people living near them or create temporary alliances with others.

Loosely organized in small bands and larger regional groups, the Comanche never fought together as a single people. Because of their fragmentary political organization they never maintained a single policy or united front. They rarely fought one another, however, and frequently their bands would join to fight against a common enemy.

The Comanche were skilled warriors and fierce soldiers, mounted on horseback and armed with bows and arrows, lances, clubs, or muskets. They had fought as foot soldiers before they acquired horses, and afterward they became superb cavalry soldiers. They could attack at great distances from their camps, thus keeping enemies away from their families. Comanche raiders would sometimes travel more than 600 miles to raid. They traveled hundreds of miles to punish enemies and acquire property. They would attack quickly and then race for home with their loot. Warfare brought them mules, horses, and captives. All were useful to the Comanche. The horses and mules were used for transportation or food. Male captives were usually put to death, but women and children would be put to work and, in time, married or adopted into the tribe. Livestock as well as captives could be traded for European metal goods, knives, needles, awls, textiles, tobacco, food, or—most important of all trade goods— guns and ammunition. The raids kept enemies at a distance from their homes and hunting grounds and thus made life more secure for the Comanche people.

Engaged in ongoing struggle, the Comanche created ways to encourage bravery and military ability. Because it was essential for Comanche survival that they keep intruders out of the Comanchería, their culture encouraged military success. The life of a warrior was an expected and worthy role for Comanche men. Comanche warriors protected the Comanche people and kept them safe and secure. Successful soldiers were respected and were rewarded with status and power. The Comanche had a formal system for honoring warriors: They awarded coups, or military honors, to soldiers according to the degree of bravery a particular act merited. Killing was not essential for displaying bravery. Simply touching a live enemy with one's hand was considered an exceptional act of courage. Rushing in among a crowd of enemy warriors and striking them with a stick or club was a very brave act. Killing an enemy from a great distance with a gun or bow and arrow did not, from the Comanche point of view, require as much courage as killing an enemy with a club or knife at close quarters. Scalping was not highly regarded by the Comanche. They took scalps—cutting around the head just below the hairline and then pulling off the entire scalp—but scalping a dead enemy was not especially honored. Scalps themselves were seen only as visible proof of Comanche success, not proof of bravery.

Captives were often treated very roughly and brutalized at first to frighten them and so control them more easily. The Comanche could not take male prisoners because they had no prisons and adult men were enemy warriors and therefore dangerous. The Comanche killed the captured men and took the women and children as prisoners. Captives were sometimes tortured, but torture was not a common practice; the personality and character of the captor determined whether his captives were tortured. Though some Comanches did mutilate and murder their captives, most Comanches would put them to work and, in time, marry or adopt the captive into their families. Others might trade them for European goods. Comanche captives who accepted the Comanche and their way of life were well treated and respected as Comanche.

When the Comanche entered the southern Plains they confronted the Indian people already living there, the Apache. The Apache were a seminomadic hunting people who had themselves come down from the north to live on the Plains several centuries earlier. They lived in bands much like the Co-

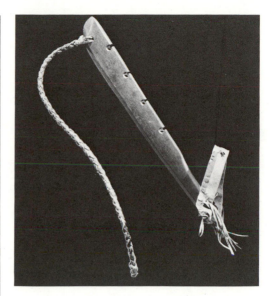

A carved wood club, called a tekniwup, *used only by Comanche war leaders. The rawhide wristband attached to the handle helped the warrior keep a tight grip, and the braided rawhide strip hanging from the top served as a whip. Such a club was both a weapon and a symbol of the leader's authority.*

manche, and their bands were loosely organized into several divisions. We know them by the names they were given by the first Europeans to come into the area, the Spanish, who knew them as the Farones, Jicarillas, Mescaleros, Palomas, Catalanas, and Lipans. These divisions, together known as the Eastern Apache, lived in band communities called *rancherías* by the Spanish. The Apaches were among the first Indians to get horses, and they, too, were buffalo hunters. Unlike the Comanche, however, they were also farmers, probably having learned from

Pueblo Indians how to practice agriculture. Their crops of corn, beans, and squash supplemented the food they gathered by hunting. Their small farm plots restricted the Apache to certain locations, for they had to stay in one area to tend their gardens. Their known locations made it possible for the Comanche to find and attack them. The Apache, hovering near their ranchería gardens, were easy targets for Comanche raiders, who began attacking the Apache in the early 18th century. The Apache bands, based on separate rancherías, fought separately, and separately they were attacked, destroyed, and driven from the land.

Operating singly or combining their forces, Comanche bands sought out and attacked the Apache. They destroyed the rancherías and stole Apache horses, women, and children. Their long and bloody campaign lasted for much of the 18th century. The Comanche drove the Farones, Palomas, Jicarillas, and Mescaleros west into the mountains of New Mexico and the Lipans south to the Rio Grande.

Although the Spanish were not directly involved in the struggle, their presence contributed to it. They were, first, the source of the horses that had quickly become essential to the Indians. Indians acquired horses by stealing and breeding them as well as by trading. The Spanish also provided metal tools and weapons that the Indians desired, but they always tried to deny Indians another important European item, the gun. Intent on conquering territory and controlling and converting the Indians, the Spanish knew that the new weapons would rapidly be turned on themselves. Mounted Indians armed with guns were formidable enemies, especially against other Indians who had neither horses nor guns. Some Indians did get a few guns, but they could not produce either the weapons themselves or gunpowder and shot. Only trade with European colonists provided Indians with guns and ammunition. Not until the 19th century did the Comanche gain easy access to guns.

The French were also interested in exploiting the wealth of North America,

European weapons, such as this late 17th century French flintlock rifle, were greatly sought after by Indians. Guns became an important bargaining tool for Europeans who wanted to control trade with strategically located Indian tribes.

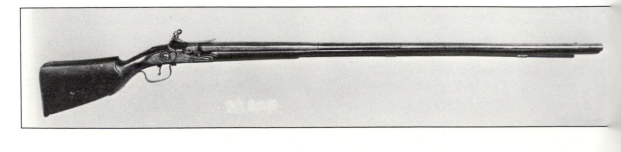

but although they had the same goals and ambitions as the Spanish they were unable to carry out their colonial policy in the same way. French people were reluctant to cross the Atlantic Ocean, and because relatively few came to settle in North America there were never enough of them to carry out a program of conquest among the Indians. Much French exploration and colonization was financed by investment companies, which were more interested in making a profit than in converting Indians to Christianity.

Lacking a significant military presence, the French were dependent on the Indians' good will and seldom made demands for Indian land. Their missions were never able to subdue large numbers of Indians and put them to work on mission farms. In Europe the French claimed to possess all of a vast area they called Louisiana, but in Louisiana itself they actually possessed only enough land to build a trading post. Seeking trade and political alliances rather than land, the French set out to make a profit by trading for the furs of North America and to keep Indian loyalty by giving the Indians what they wanted for their furs. Indians wanted guns, and the French were willing to provide them. Guns encouraged trade because they were desirable enough to encourage the Indians to trade in the first place. Because the guns were useless without French powder and shot, the Indians returned to trade and maintained their friendship with the French.

The French were eager to exploit new territory and prevent their British and Spanish rivals from gaining control of the country. In the 17th century French trappers, traders, and missionaries traveled from the east to the Great Lakes and followed the nearby rivers west. In 1673 the French trader Louis Jolliet and the Jesuit priest Jacques Marquette traveled down the Mississippi River as far south as the mouth of the Arkansas River. In 1683 the explorer and entrepreneur René-Robert Cavelier, Sieur de la Salle, traveled even further down the Mississippi. La Salle reached the river's mouth at the Gulf of Mexico and claimed all the land drained by the great river as a possession of France. When he returned to France he convinced the French king, Louis XIV, to establish an outpost there, arguing that a French post would secure control of the Mississippi River valley and the interior of the continent and provide an ice-free port for French settlements in Canada. With an outpost on the Gulf Coast the French could prevent British expansion into the interior and keep watch over the nearby Spanish as well.

In 1684 La Salle returned to the New World and established a French settlement on the Gulf Coast of Texas, but it survived for less than a year. Although it was a failure for the French, its presence convinced the Spanish to establish the first Spanish settlement in Texas, a mission on the Neces River, in 1690. In 1693, when the Spanish saw that the French were no longer a threat, they abandoned that mission.

The French, however, remained interested in the West. They had established a small outpost at the mouth of the Arkansas River in 1692, and in 1699 and 1702 French priests established two missions among the Indians of Illinois, at Cahokia and further south, across the Mississippi River from present-day St. Louis, Missouri. In 1700 a French expedition sailed to the Gulf Coast and established a settlement at Biloxi. French soldiers and traders from Canada and the Gulf posts began traveling on the great rivers that flowed from the West. In 1713, Louis Juchereau de Saint-Denis went up the Red River and established a French trading post among the Caddoan Indians at Natchitoches. Eager to establish trade with the Spanish of New Mexico, he crossed Texas to San Juan Bautista, a Spanish mission and *presidio*, or fort, on the Rio Grande the following year.

Saint-Denis's surprising appearance at San Juan Bautista convinced the Spanish once again to move northeast to stop the French intrusion. In 1716 they sent soldiers and priests into south Texas and established a presidio and mission on the Neces. In 1718 they established another mission on the San Antonio River in Texas. Within a few years there was a string of missions and presidios across southern Texas from the Rio Grande to the edge of French Louisiana. Indians living in the region were persuaded and sometimes forced to come to the missions to work on the Spaniards' farms. The Texas missions were never entirely successful, for the

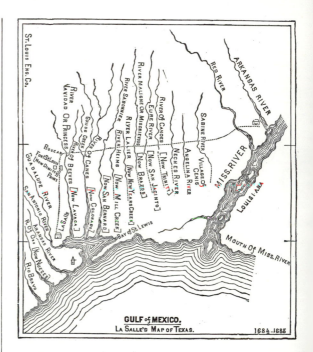

Map drawn in 1684 by French explorer René-Robert Cavelier, Sieur de la Salle, showing the land he claimed for France when he explored what is now the Gulf Coast of Texas. The map text gives the new Spanish and English names of rivers and other sites, reflecting France's inability to maintain its land claims in North America.

Indians were not eager to become Roman Catholics or farmers. Despite this lack of success, the missions and forts remained in Texas to keep the French from moving into Spanish territory.

In 1719 two French explorers went west. Bernard de la Harpe went up the Red River. Somewhere beyond the Great Bend he left the river and traveled north to a great Wichita Indian village on the Canadian River in what is now eastern Oklahoma. That same year

Claude Charles du Tisné went into what is now eastern Kansas and traded with the Caddoan-speaking Indians living there. The French sought trade with the Plains Indians and, believing that New Mexico was a place of great wealth, with the Spanish there as well. The French went among the Indians and provided trade goods, textiles (principally woolens), metal tools, knives, awls, needles, hoes, pots, pans, and guns. Seeking access to New Mexico and friendly relations and trade with the Indians along the way, French traders went up the Red, the Arkansas, the Missouri, and the Kansas rivers into the West and out onto the Great Plains.

The Indians living on the Plains welcomed the French traders because their merchandise was desirable. In the north Indians traded animal furs, principally beaver, for the French items. But the beaver pelts that the Indians farther south could provide were less desirable. Because the winters were so mild the animals never produced thick pelts. These Indians, forced to produce other items that the French wanted, brought in dried meat, buffalo hides, and deerskins. They soon discovered that the French were also willing to trade for horses and mules as well as Indian captives to use as laborers.

The French gave the Indians guns and ammunition along with knives, pots, pans, blankets, and other trade items. In order to continue acquiring these goods, the Indians had to continue to provide what the French wanted. Once the Indians had hunted all the animals from their own lands, they were forced to invade and hunt on other Indians' land. French trade, fueled by the guns, thus contributed to violence in Indian country. Indians armed with French guns drove others from their land and secured better hunting territory that would produce more game, more furs, and more captives.

The Comanche, living between the frontiers of Spanish and French territory, had access to both Spanish horses and French guns. Although they always had more horses than guns, the combination made the Comanche particularly powerful among the Plains In-

In 1718 the Spanish began to build the San Jose Mission, the second structure erected in Comanche Territory. It was four miles south of the city of San Antonio and took several years to complete. The Spanish built many more across what is now the state of Texas in the hope of keeping control of the region.

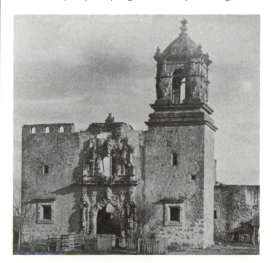

dians. They had need of their power, for in the 18th century they were surrounded by aggressive Indians. The Pawnee were a large tribe that always posed a threat to the Comanche in the north, where both competed for the buffalo. To the northeast, the Osage, although less numerous than the Comanche, had greater access to French guns. They also had horses, acquired

A European mirror from the 1860s. The French traded such luxury items as well as guns, ammunition, and metal objects to the Indians in exchange for hides and furs.

through theft and trade with the Wichita. Always better armed than the Comanche, the Osage roamed and hunted in the Arkansas and Canadian river valleys and remained a threat until the 1830s. East of the Comanche were the Wichita and other groups of Caddoan-speaking peoples. Although the Comanche occasionally fought with these people, for the most part they maintained peace with them. There was a practical reason for doing so: The French came up the Red River to trade at Wichita villages, and that was where the Comanche could acquire the guns they needed to fight the Apache, Pawnee, and Osage. The Wichita established two large villages, located near present-day Rowland, Texas, that served as a trading center. This location, which mistakenly came to be known as Spanish Fort, was important for Comanche trade throughout the 18th century. They brought horses, mules, hides, meat, and Apache captives that they exchanged for Wichita corn and beans and French metal tools and weapons.

South of the Wichita were several smaller tribes of Caddoan-speaking people, the Waco and Kichais. The Tonkawa, always a threat to the Comanche, lived farther to the south. They fought with the Comanche for most of the 18th and 19th centuries as both competed for hunting territory in central Texas.

To the south and west lived various groups of Apache. In the south the Lipan Apache were constant threats to the Comanche, as were the Mescalero,

Jicarilla, Palomas, and Farone Apache to the west. The Apache and Comanche were almost always at war with one another.

North of the Comanche lived the Ute. Although a distantly related people with whom the Comanche had been friendly in the early 18th century, the two became rivals later in that century. They fought one another for years, competing for horses and buffalo as well as access to the goods of the Pueblo Indians and Spaniards of New Mexico.

As the Europeans' presence increased, their demands for pelts led to increased hunting by the Indians. Tribes competed to control the resources of the southern Plains. Guns and horses encouraged the competition and gave mobility and power to the Indian warfare. Indians became locked in a bitter and bloody struggle against each other for survival.

The Comanche did not have a unified or consistent policy toward the Spanish. Their bands in the north and west were near the Spanish of New Mexico, while the bands in the south were near the Spanish of Texas. The northern and western bands would sometimes rob the Spanish as well as the Pueblo Indians of New Mexico, taking cattle, horses, mules, and captives for food and trade, but at other times they left off raiding in favor of peace and trade. In retaliation for Comanche raids the Spanish, aided by Pueblo warriors, searched them out on the Plains. Occasionally their efforts met with suc-

cess, but more often they were failures, for the highly mobile Comanche were hard to find and defeat.

But there were times when the Comanche felt it was tactically advisable to be at peace with the Spanish and Pueblo Indians, who held fairs at which other Indians could trade for food, tobacco, cloth, blankets, metal tools, and livestock. The trade fairs held at the Taos and Pecos pueblos were the most important, but there were others as well. The Comanche came to the fairs in northern New Mexico and traded their buffalo hides, deerskins, buffalo robes, and dried meat for corn, tobacco, knives, horses, and mules. The Comanche also brought to the trade fairs the Spaniards and Indians who they had captured in the south. They traded these captives to the Spanish of New Mexico, who always purchased the freedom of Spanish prisoners and tried to secure that of Indian captives also. Unfortunately, this encouraged the Comanche to take even more prisoners.

Comanche trade was important to the economy of New Mexico, whose settlers and Indians alike needed the meat and hides brought in by the Plains people. The Spanish also had political reasons for encouraging this trade relationship: They believed that by maintaining friendly relations with the Plains Indians, especially the Comanche, who controlled the region between French Louisiana and Spanish New Mexico, they could keep the French out of the region. They also believed both that trade would create friendship and bring an end to the frequent Comanche raids and that regulating trade would give them some control over these Indians.

Trade for the Spanish goods on which they were increasingly dependent was important to the Comanche, but they were also more than willing to take what they wanted by raiding the Pueblos and the Spanish. For most of the 18th century the Comanche relationship with the Spanish and Pueblos was an uneasy one, with periods of peace interrupted by outbreaks of theft and violence.

The relationship of the southern Comanche bands with the Spanish of Texas, on the other hand, was unremittingly hostile. The Lipan Apache, driven south by the hammering attacks of the Comanche, approached the Spanish of San Antonio and asked for protection. The Lipans wanted the Spaniards to establish a mission in the north, where they could be sheltered from the Comanche. Because some Spanish had settled further north, in 1757 the Spanish set up a mission and a presidio to protect the settlers along the San Saba River. This mission attracted only a few Apache, but its presence convinced the Comanche that the Spanish were helping their enemies. In March 1758 about 2,000 Comanche, Wichitas, and other Caddoan-speaking Indians arrived at the mission. They talked the Spanish priests into allowing them to enter the walled compound. Once inside, the Comanche and their allies lashed out at the people gathered

there, killing most of the inhabitants and looting the mission.

This was the first Comanche attack in the south, but it was not the last. The next year the Spanish sent out an expedition led by Colonel Diego Ortiz Parilla to punish the Comanche and the Wichita. Soldiers from the presidios of San Saba and Bexar and about 200 friendly Indians went north looking for the Comanche and the Wichita. Unable to find the Comanche, Parilla led his force to the Wichita villages on the Red River, where the Comanche were indeed hiding. The Indians, whose villages were surrounded by large walls of mounded earth, remained inside. Parilla fired his cannons at the walls but could not destroy them. Unable to punish the Indians, he returned to San Antonio. The Comanche and Wichita left the forts and followed close behind. They attacked Parilla and turned the expedition's return into a rout.

In time the Comanche extended their reach beyond the Spaniards and Indians in New Mexico and Texas. They began raiding farther south, deep into Mexico, to get livestock, captives, and other loot to exchange with the Wichita and French traders on the Red River or the Spanish and Pueblo Indians at Taos, Pecos, or Santa Fe.

When the Spanish were at peace with a group of Comanche, they were convinced that they had made peace with all of the Comanche. The Comanche, however, had a different notion. Each band was independent of the others. No one Comanche could speak for another. A particularly influential band leader might be able to control his band, but he could never control any of the other Comanche bands. Also, western bands might in good faith establish peace with the Spanish of New Mexico, yet continue to raid the Spanish in Texas and Mexico; southern bands might make peace with the Spanish of Texas and raid in New Mexico. They were not being dishonest or treacherous: They made peace on an individual or band basis with other individuals or communities. As they lacked overall tribal unity, they did not recognize the unity of the Spanish. They believed that each band was justified in attacking and stealing from any group of people with whom it had not established peace. The Spanish were also practicing a kind of double-dealing: Those in New Mexico continued to trade with the Comanche, knowing full well that the horses and captives came from the Spanish in Texas and Mexico. They valued their own peace more than they valued the safety and peace of their compatriots in the south. A full mutual understanding of what peaceful relations involved was particularly difficult for two groups that did not share the same ideas about political power, peace, and war.

In 1763 the French were defeated by the English in Canada and were forced to leave North America. The Comanche and other Plains Indians missed the French, for now Louisiana to the east was not controlled by the friendly French traders but by the Spanish. After 1763, although Euro-American

Drawing by a Spaniard of a Yamparika Comanche. His bow, quiver of arrows, and lance are typical of Indian culture, but his lance has a metal tip acquired through trade with Europeans; his arrows may also be metal-tipped. The metal ax and flintlock rifle are probably French or Spanish.

traders still went into the West from Louisiana, the trading balance was changed. The new traders, now in Spanish territory, offered fewer guns. Now there were Spaniards on both sides of the Comanchería, and the Comanche faced a more consistent trade policy. Fortunately for them, the Spanish feared to anger the Indians of Louisiana, who were accustomed to the gun trade, so they continued the French

THIS MEMORIAL IS THE
PROPERTY OF THE STATE OF COLORADO

IN THIS VICINITY THE COMANCHE CHIEF

CUERNO VERDE
(GREENHORN)

THE "CRUEL SCOURGE", WAS DEFEATED
AND KILLED BY THE SPANIARDS UNDER
GOV. JUAN B. ANZA ON SEPT. 3, 1779.
THE NEARBY MOUNTAIN AND STREAM
TAKE THEIR NAME FROM THE CHIEF.
ANZA'S WAS THE FIRST EXPEDITION
THROUGH CERTAIN PARTS OF COLORADO.

ERECTED BY
THE STATE HISTORICAL SOCIETY OF COLORADO
FROM
THE MRS. J. N. HALL FOUNDATION
AND BY
STATE CIVIL SERVICE EMPLOYEES OF COLORADO
1932

This stone memorial marks the spot where the Comanche chief Cuerno Verde was killed in a 1779 attack by Spanish officer Don Juan Bautista de Anza. The attack was the first successful European penetration of the Comanchería.

policy of trading guns and ammunition to the Indians. Some of these guns eventually found their way west, and so the Comanche were still able to acquire some weapons and trade goods.

Starting in the late 1760s the Spanish began to reorganize their frontiers in New Mexico and Texas, sending several able colonial administrators there. One was Don Juan Bautista De Anza, a very talented officer, who was sent to New Mexico in 1777. To end the Comanche raids, De Anza believed, it was necessary to pursue them into the Comanchería and attack them there. Earlier

Spanish leaders had tried to do this without success, but De Anza accomplished his goal. Aided by the Ute and Apache, he led Spanish troops into the northern part of the Comanchería in the summer of 1779 and came upon a group of Comanche. De Anza attacked them, and in the course of the battle he killed an important Comanche war leader, Cuerno Verde (Green Horn).

In 1780 and 1781 an outbreak of smallpox killed a large number of Comanche. They were weakened by the loss of their people. They now had fewer guns and inadequate ammunition because they were trading less with the Spanish than they previously had with the French. The Comanche feared attack by better-armed eastern tribes with English guns, as well as another attack from De Anza. In 1785 a group of western Comanche went to Taos and asked the Spanish for peace. About the same time a group of Penateka and Kotsoteka leaders went to San Antonio and requested peace and trade with the Spanish there.

De Anza met with the Comanche at Taos in 1786. He demanded that the western Comanche select one leader to represent them all. The Comanche were reluctant to create a single leader, but they finally chose a prominent war chief, called by the Spanish Ecueracapa (Leather Jacket), to speak for them. The Comanche agreed to stop warring on the Spanish of New Mexico in exchange for peace and trade. Eager to end the violence, the Spanish agreed to trade once again with the Comanche. The Comanche and Spanish made peace in 1786 and remained at peace for the next 50 years. The Comanche continued their century-long fight against the Apache with Spanish approval and help. Now when the Apache attacked the Spanish, the Comanche joined the Spanish on raiding expeditions against them. The Comanche continued to attend the trade fairs of New Mexico, and Spanish and Pueblo traders went out and exchanged goods with the Comanche on the Plains. These New Mexico traders, known as the Comancheros, continued to trade with the Comanche into the late 19th century. While the Comanche fought the Anglos (settlers of English or northern European origin) in Texas, Spanish traders continued to travel safely among the Comanche and conduct trade.

The Spanish kept their agreement of peace. In the late 1780s, when drought drove many of the buffalo away from the Comanchería, the Spanish sent food to the Comanche. The Spanish also joined the Comanche on raids against their enemies, the Pawnee. In 1795 the Spanish engineered an important peace agreement between the Comanche and their immediate neighbors to the north, the Kiowa and Kiowa-Apache. The Kiowa then posed no threat to the Comanche, and now all fought together against the Pawnee and the Osage.

Because Ecueracapa spoke only for the western Comanche, the peace he established with De Anza did not apply to the Spanish of Texas. The Spanish in Texas, unable to pursue and punish the Comanche, were forced to endure Comanche raids. The Comanche robbed them of their horses and livestock and took the animals either to New Mexico to trade for food and European goods, or to the east, to trade for guns to fight the Apache, Ute, Pawnee, and Osage.

Through the 18th century, the Comanche held on to the Comanchería. They created alliances and animosity. They struggled with other Indians and established relations with non-Indian newcomers. They were able to conquer several groups of Indians and held both the French and Spanish at bay. As the century came to an end, pressure on the Comanche and their land continued as existing and potential enemies grew in numbers and strength. Even so, the Comanche remained the rulers of the southern Plains. ▲

Comanches on the Warpath, *painted by Theodore Gentilz in 1896, shows the flat grasslands and stands of trees that made up the Comanchería.*

MASTERS
OF THE
COMANCHERÍA

In the last years of the late 18th century Spain became involved in wars in Europe and began to neglect its frontier settlements in North America. With fewer troops and funds the border communities in Texas and northern Mexico were left defenseless. The settlers there, to whom the Peace of 1786 did not apply, remained subject to Comanche raids and suffered tremendously.

Every spring, as warm weather began to return and the Comanche were assured of ample grass for their horses, they left their camps in New Mexico and headed south. After 1790 the Comanche were joined by their new allies, the Kiowa, and together the raiders from both tribes rode south to steal cattle and horses. The Spanish defenses in northern Mexico continued to deteriorate, and the Comanche began raiding deeper and deeper into Mexico and drove away thousands of horses and mules.

As conditions in Europe led to greater political instability in North America, the Comanche enjoyed increased prosperity and success. Mexico, which achieved independence from Spain in 1821, was no better able to protect its northern outposts. Comanche raids there continued well into the early 19th century.

Meanwhile, the United States had secured its independence from Great Britain and in 1803 purchased the Louisiana Territory from France. Now a unified nation whose government was based in North America became the new neighbor of the Comanche. Despite this new power on its eastern border, there was little change in the Comanchería. The old French and Spanish traders from Missouri and Louisiana continued to visit them along the Red River, and in time Anglo-American traders visited them as well. The Comanche were willing to trade with any-

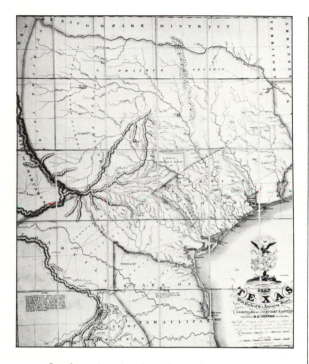

Stephen Austin, for whom Austin, Texas, is named, drew this map of the colony of Texas in 1830. Austin was the colony's administrator. His wealth and influential contacts contributed to the success of the Texas Revolution of 1835, in which the colony became an independent republic.

one, so they met with the newcomers and exchanged their horses and mules for manufactured goods.

In the 1820s American colonizers began bringing settlers into Mexican Texas. The Mexicans hoped that these American colonies would serve as a barrier to keep the Comanche away from the Mexican communities of northern Mexico and so did not prevent the colonization of Texas. Within a few years, several thousand Anglo-Americans had

arrived, largely through the efforts of colonizers such as Haden Edwards, Green DeWitt and Stephen Austin. The settlers had little contact with the Comanche. Most of their communities were east of the Colorado River, outside of the Comanchería and out of the path of Comanche raiders on their way to Mexico. The Comanche continued their southern raids and largely ignored the Anglo-Texas settlements. On one occasion, Stephen Austin was captured by a group of Comanche raiders while on a trip to Mexico City, but they let him and his horses go and took only his Spanish grammar book. Austin was unharmed.

After purchasing Louisiana, the United States decided to move the Indians living in the east to land west of the Mississippi in order to open up eastern lands for white settlers. Even before this removal policy became official through legislation, the federal government convinced some tribes that relocating in the West would help them escape the pressure of white settlement. In 1830 Congress passed the Indian Removal Act, and the government began forcing thousands of eastern Indians to move west. Indians were moved to an area known as the Indian Territory, a region in present-day eastern Oklahoma and Kansas and western Missouri and Arkansas. Thousands of Cherokee, Delaware, Kickapoo, Shawnee, and other eastern tribes moved to the prairies, and they began hunting on the southern Plains. The buffalo they killed were from herds that the Comanche believed were theirs. To protect their major food source, the Comanche fought the Indian newcomers whenever they met them.

At about the same time, Anglo traders began crossing the northern part of the Comanchería. In 1821 William Becknell, a Missouri trader, left Missouri with several wagonloads of goods to trade with the Comanche. Before he reached them, however, he learned that Mexico had achieved its independence from Spain. Becknell quickly changed his plans and headed west to Santa Fe, where he was greeted warmly by the New Mexicans. Living on the extreme northern frontier of Mexico, New Mexicans had little access to manufactured goods and were eager to trade with Becknell. The Santa Fe trade proved so profitable that a steady stream of Missouri traders soon began traveling west every year. To reach Santa Fe, their wagon trains had to cross the northern Comanchería.

The intrusions to the north and east disturbed the Comanche. They seldom attacked the Santa Fe wagons, but they determinedly fought the eastern Indians. The U.S. government, making efforts to convince many eastern Indians to move west, feared that Comanche violence in Indian Territory would give eastern tribes good reason to refuse to move there. The government sent delegations in 1832 and 1833 to meet with the Indians and establish peace between the Comanche and the eastern tribes. These first expeditions were unable to find the Comanche, and the United States did not have its first official contact with them until 1834.

That summer a group of soldiers left Fort Gibson on the Arkansas River, military headquarters of the Indian Territory, and somewhere north of present-day Fort Sill they found a Wichita village. Colonel Henry Dodge, leader of the expedition, convinced the Wichita to take his party to the Comanche, and in July the Americans met with the Comanche. George Catlin, an artist who was traveling with the expedition, sketched the Indians, and his drawings have provided us with some of the earliest pictures of the Comanche. This first official meeting between the Comanche and the U.S. government was peaceful. The Comanche and the Wichita were willing to make peace with the Americans and claimed that they were ready to make peace with the eastern tribes. The Comanche, however, refused Dodge's request that they go back beyond the Cross Timbers to meet with the other tribes at Fort Gibson. They did, however, meet with some Osage who had accompanied Dodge. The Osage, a prairie tribe that had been pushed farther west by the arrival of eastern tribes, had for years fought against both the Comanche and Kiowa. Because the Osage returned two Kiowa children whom they had captured in an earlier raid, the Comanche, Wichita, and a group of Kiowa who were also at the meeting agreed to make peace with the Osage.

The next summer a group of Comanche and Wichita met with U.S. government representatives at Camp Holmes, a post along the Canadian River in the Cross Timbers. At this meeting they promised to keep the peace and share their hunting territory with the eastern tribes. Only a few Comanche were at the Camp Holmes meeting, but even so, relationships among some of the Indians improved. The Camp Holmes meeting confirmed the agreement with the Osage reached the previous year. After the meetings, the Comanche agreed to meet and trade with the Osage, who had access to merchandise from eastern traders.

For the next 20 years, in late July or early August, the Osage brought manufactured goods to the Great Salt Plain between the Arkansas and Cimarron rivers. The Comanche drove thousands of horses and mules to this plain, where they traded them for guns, ammunition, and other goods. The Osage took the horses and mules to Missouri and Arkansas and traded them to Americans. This lucrative trade guaranteed the peace between these old rivals, and both groups enjoyed the benefits of it for years.

Although the Comanche resented the presence of the eastern Indians on their borders, they attacked those Indians only when they ventured onto the Comanchería. The Comanche did not believe that the American newcomers crossing their land were a serious

An 1844 etching shows a wagon train carrying traders to Santa Fe in what is now the state of New Mexico. Militia on horseback accompanied travelers to protect them from attacks by the Comanche and other Plains Indians.

threat, and they knew they were potential trading partners, so they largely
ignored the Anglo-Americans and seldom raided the wagons crossing to
Santa Fe.

Anglo settlers in Texas, however,
were definitely considered a threat. The
early Anglo-Texans did not move into
central Texas and were not in the path
of Comanche raiders on their way to
Mexico. In time, however, more and
more settlers began moving to Comanche fringe areas, where they became
subject to attacks. The settlers brought
livestock, including a new breed of
horse that was stronger and larger. The
Texas settlers did not travel or settle together but instead moved west in family groups and settled on small, isolated
farms at a distance from one another.

These settlers, possessing attractive
livestock and living alone on isolated
farms, were soon prime targets of Comanche attacks. Their raids on Anglo-
Texas settlements began around 1835.
At the time, Texans were involved in
their brief war for independence from
Mexico, and they focused little atten-
tion on the Comanche raiders until they
defeated the Mexicans the following
year.

In 1836 Texas became an independent country and established its own
Indian policy. Texan leaders David Bur-
nett and Sam Houston attempted to
make peace with the Comanche. Houston, who had lived for years among the
Cherokee, was sympathetic to the Comanche. He believed that if they were
treated honorably and honestly by Tex-

General Sam Houston, one of the few U.S.
government officials who argued for fair
treatment of the Comanche. He served twice
as president of the Republic of Texas, where
he had originally been sent to make treaties
with the Indian tribes of the region.

ans, they would respond by maintaining peaceful relations. Houston sent
several delegates to the Comanchería to
request meetings, and several Comanche leaders traveled to San Antonio. A
peace agreement was drawn up by the
two sides. The Indians wanted the
whites to stay out of the Comanchería
and out of their way when they went
south to raid in Mexico. Houston was
unable to guarantee that whites would
stay out of Comanche country, but he
did promise to establish trading posts
among the Comanche in exchange for

peace. Houston's agreement was not approved by the Senate of Texas and trading posts were not established. The Texans did little to convince the Comanche of their good intentions.

After Texas's independence more Americans moved there. The Texas Republic, eager to attract settlers, began offering 1,280 acres of free land to all new arrivals. There was an economic crisis in the United States in 1837, and to avoid unemployment and poverty thousands of newcomers flooded into Texas and began moving west into Comanche country. To protect their land, the Comanche attacked the settlers. Now free of other military responsibilities, Texans formed local military units and groups of Indian fighters to protect their people and drive the Indians away. The Texas Rangers, which had been organized in 1836 to protect the Texans from Indians, began fighting the Comanche.

These Texas fighters soon discovered, as the Spanish had in 18th-century New Mexico, that the best way to end Comanche onslaughts was to pursue the raiders back to their homeland and attack them there. Comanche raids were followed by retaliatory attacks by the Texans. In 1839 a group of Texans, guided by some Lipan Apache, surprised a Comanche camp near the mouth of the San Saba River and killed a number of them.

The Texans' attacks within the Comanchería were so successful that in early 1840 three Comanche leaders came to San Antonio and asked to make peace. In March of the same year 65 more Comanches came to San Antonio to negotiate a peace agreement. Twelve of the leaders, led by their spokesman, Muguara, the most important band leader, went inside the Council House while the women, children, and other men waited in the square in front of the building.

The Texans demanded the return of all white captives held by the Comanche. Muguara had brought in one white woman and claimed that he had no more captives. He was probably telling the truth, for captives belonged to the individuals who took them, and not to the tribe as a whole. Although other Comanche bands surely held captives, Muguara had no power to make them turn their prisoners over to the Texans. Comanche leaders could rarely force even members of their own bands to return captives, and they certainly could not return captives held by other bands. It was simply impossible.

The Texans refused to believe Muguara and, bringing a group of armed soldiers into the council room, announced that Muguara and his men would be held hostage until all the whites had been returned. At this, the Comanches jumped up and tried to escape but were shot by the soldiers as they fled the room. Some fought their way out with knives and continued fighting outside the Council House. The fight was a brief one. When it was over the Texans had killed all 12 of the Comanche leaders and 23 of the others and made prisoners of the 27 surviving

(continued on page 73)

MADE ON THE COMANCHERÍA

Riding horses, hunting buffalo and other game, and keeping intruders out of their vast territory, the Comanche lived off the resources of the Plains. Everything they needed they made themselves or got through trade.

Like people everywhere, the Comanche decorated the objects they made and used. They used vegetable dyes and powdered colored stones and earths to paint on rawhide and tanned leather. They attached colorful feathers and other animal parts such as deer hooves to the things they made. These decorations usually symbolized protection by a spirit power or represented an actual event.

When people of European origin began to cross the Comanchería, the Comanche traded buffalo hides to them in exchange for cloth, beads, firearms, and metal weapons and tools. Some of the new materials improved the function of traditional objects, such as the sharp, long-lasting metal tips that replaced stone points on shields and arrows. Other new materials added to the visual appeal of traditional objects, such as the colorful pieces of cloth and beading added to shields and containers.

Only late in the 19th century, when the Comanche were all living on a reservation, would they cease to make the things they had used when they were horse-riding hunters, raiders, and traders on the Plains.

Steel-tipped lance that belonged to the warrior White Eagle, about 1870. Hawk and peacock feathers are attached to the red cloth cover.

The Comanche Yoke-Suite made this painting on buckskin to record the 1874 Comanche-Kiowa-Cheyenne attack on white buffalo hunters at Adobe Walls, Texas. The hunters' rifles send bursts of fire from the stockade as Indians attack with arrows. The light blue areas represent the South Canadian River and a creek; the green represents trees and the bluffs overlooking the river. At top right a Cheyenne riding a white horse is killed; at left (detail, above) a Comanche lies dead. A wounded Comanche and a Kiowa ride together on the horse at bottom center. At bottom right, Quanah Parker dismounts from his white horse and thrusts his lance at a hunter concealed in a wagon, accounting for one of the three casualties among the whites. The Indians' weapons were no match for the hunters' long-range firearms, and dozens were killed.

A saddle frame of the traditional type, made of wood and deerhorn and covered with rawhide. A saddle blanket would have been placed over the seat frame.

Braided-thong whip with bone handle.

A man's saddle from the mid-19th century. The wood frame and stirrups are covered with rawhide. The buffalo-skin stirrup straps were tied to adjust their length.

A woman's saddle made around 1850 of wood covered with rawhide. The decorative fringe is tanned leather.

Outside of a buckskin shield cover. The red-and-blue lines pointing toward the center represent rifles.

Inside of a buckskin shield cover. Red cloth and white feathers are attached. The designs represent white people, a building, and various animals.

Inside (above) and outside (right) of
a buckskin shield cover. At the center
of the inside is a many-pointed star;
the circle design at the top represents
the peyote button. The cover and its
shield were made in the mid-19th
century.

A fur quiver trimmed with beading and deer-skin, and the arrows carried in it.

Outside of a shield cover, made of yellow-dyed buckskin. Attached to it are horsehair wrapped in red cloth, hawk feathers (at right), and deer hooves with an eagle feather.

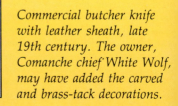

Commercial butcher knife with leather sheath, late 19th century. The owner, Comanche chief White Wolf, may have added the carved and brass-tack decorations.

(continued from page 64)

Comanche women and children. The massacre of their people at San Antonio enraged the Comanche and convinced them that it was useless to talk with the whites, for the Texans could not be trusted.

Shortly afterward a southern Comanche leader, Isomania, rode into San Antonio alone and challenged the Texans to fight him. The residents of San Antonio remained inside their homes and refused to meet his challenge. Isomania then took his warriors to the Mission San José where the Comanche prisoners were being held and demanded their release. However, the soldiers holding the prisoners remained inside the stone walls of the mission and refused to speak with the Comanche. Disgusted with the Texans, Isomania and his band rode away.

The Council House Massacre was followed by a series of retaliatory attacks by the Comanche, and a pattern of raid and retaliation began anew. In August a large group of Comanche attacked and raided Texas settlements all the way to the Gulf Coast. Texans pursued the Comanche and defeated them along Plum Creek. Texas Rangers, soldiers, and local militia continued to go after the Comanche, following them into the Comanchería and attacking them there. No longer were the Comanche safe in the heart of the Comanchería. Two months after Plum Creek a group of Texans and Lipan Apache surprised a Comanche village deep in the Comanchería, near present-day Colorado, Texas. They killed more than 130 Comanche and captured more than 500 horses. To stop the attacks in the Comanchería, the Comanche gave Texans a brief period of peace and directed most of their raids against the Mexicans south of the Rio Grande.

This peace was brief because settlers continued to arrive. The Republic of Texas was eager to have settlements throughout its territory and began advertising in Europe for settlers. During the early 1840s thousands of Germans and Irish poured into Texas, settling in the west and north, closer than earlier settlers to the Comanchería. The Comanche continued to concentrate their raids on Mexico, but as more whites moved west they came within range of Comanche raids. Throughout this period representatives of the Texas government attempted to meet and negotiate with the Comanche, but the Indians, remembering the treachery of the Council House, were reluctant to come in to talk with the Texans. In 1843 several Texas agents traveled north and met with a large group of the Penateka band. Some Comanche wanted to kill the whites, but their leaders convinced them to respect the flag of truce and after listening to the Texan's proposals to let the delegates go.

In 1844, Sam Houston, the president of Texas, met with a group of Comanche at Tehuacana Creek. The Comanche once again agreed to make peace if the Texans would stay out of their land. Houston knew that he could neither stop the tide of white settlers nor guarantee the Comanche any land, and without such promises no peace agreement would last. There were some agreements: Promises were made on both sides but neither side was able to keep them. Whites intruded into the Comanchería, the Comanches raided, and violence continued along the Comanche-Texas frontier.

In 1845 the Republic of Texas became one of the United States. In the next 3 years, 70,000 people moved into Texas, many of them migrating west and settling near the Comanche. At the same time thousands of eastern Indians who had been removed to the West continued to hunt in the territory of the northern Comanche. The Comanche lashed out against all invaders, but now it was the responsibility of the federal government to deal with them. U.S. government representatives, in hopes of securing peace in the north and the south, met with some of the Comanche in 1846.

At this meeting, the southern Comanche agreed to remain at peace with the United States, stop all raids, return all stolen property, give up all their captives, and trade with only those traders licensed by the government. In return the government promised to keep whites out of Comanche territory, establish trading posts for the Comanche, and send blacksmiths to repair their guns and tools. This treaty, like the ones before it, was not observed by either side. The United States could not guarantee land for the Comanche in

A drawing of the Council House Fight. Texas soldiers massacred Comanche chiefs who had come to San Antonio in 1840 to negotiate a peace treaty. This action convinced the Indians that attempts to deal with the Texans were futile and led them to raid Texas communities in retaliation.

Texas, for this state entered the Union under very special circumstances.

Texas had been a part of Mexico but in 1836 successfully defeated the Mexican army and gained its independence. It had been an independent nation for almost 10 years and, when it finally did enter the union in 1845, several problems due to its special status remained. Texas had a national debt of $10 million and claimed control of land as far west as the Rio Grande. There were people living along the Rio Grande who did not accept Texas's interpretation of the boundary and insisted that the land belonged to New Mexico. A compromise was created in a series of bills passed by Congress. The United States agreed to pay the republic's debt and allow the state to keep all of its land in return for accepting a new boundary to be drawn several miles east of the Rio Grande. As a result of this agreement, the land in Texas was legally owned by the state, and therefore the federal government could not grant any of the land to the Comanche. For their part, Texans absolutely refused to give up any of their land to the Indians. So despite the promises of 1846, whites continued to trespass on Comanche lands, and the Comanche responded with violence.

In 1848 gold was discovered in California, and by 1849 thousands of adventurers were crossing the United States on their way to the goldfields. Many traveled by a northern route along the Santa Fe Trail and the Canadian River. Thousands more passed through south Texas on their way to

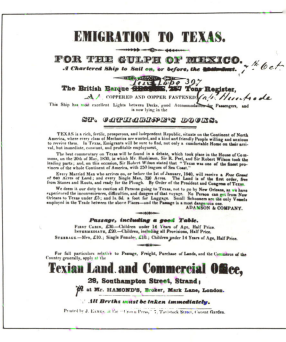

This 1839 advertisement offers free land in Texas to citizens of England. Flyers like this were posted in many European cities as the Republic of Texas attempted to increase its non-Indian population.

southern California. These travelers crossed the southern Comanchería, killing Comanche game, disrupting the seasonal movement of the buffalo, and using precious wood, water, and grass—all vital to Comanche survival. The Comanche resented this new wave of invaders, called forty-niners, who consumed their limited resources and disrupted their lives, and they attacked the newcomers.

The gold-seekers did further damage to the Indians by bringing diseases with them. In 1849 the Comanche were attacked by epidemics of cholera and

San Antonio in the 1850s. The ratio of non-Indians to Indians grew sharply after Texas became a republic in 1836 and continued to increase after Texas became a state in 1845.

smallpox, which were especially devastating to the Comanche, who had kept outsiders away from their land and had never been exposed to the diseases. The Comanche had therefore escaped the severe episodes of European diseases that struck many other Indian groups and now had no immunity to them at all. After the invasion of the Comanchería in the 19th century, cholera and smallpox killed hundreds of Comanche, including almost all of the leaders of the southern Penateka bands.

As whites poured into Texas they began pushing other Texas Indians out onto Comanche territory. Settlers drove the Tonkawa, Waco, and Wichita bands west. At the same time Kickapoo, Delaware, Shawnee, Cherokee, and other removed tribes continued to hunt on Comanche land in the northeast and kill Comanche buffalo, deer, and other game. With increased white intrusions and Indian invasions the Comanche had to compete for a diminishing supply of buffalo. Although thousands of buffalo remained, there were clearly no longer enough for all of the Indians and all of the whites. The Comanche required buffalo for food, clothing, and shelter and could not allow others to take away the source of their livelihood. They attacked the people who invaded their land, killed their buffalo, and threatened their lives.

In 1849 the government created a line of forts across Texas to protect white settlers. Beginning in the north at the Cross Timbers, the government built a series of forts reaching south to the Rio Grande to act as a barrier between white settlers and the Comanche. These early forts provided some protection for the whites and encouraged them to move deeper into Comanche territory. Within two years settlement had passed the barrier of forts and in 1851 the government had to set up a new line of forts in the west. In 1853 government representatives met once again with some of the Comanche to seek peace. Both sides agreed that peace and mutual respect were better than war. But once again little was accomplished, as neither side lived up to the treaty.

In 1855 federal agents finally convinced the Texans to cede some lands to establish a reservation system for the thousands of Indians in the state. The reservation system was a revival of an old idea of how to deal with Indian peoples. Some Americans believed that there were only two ways to end the conflict between Indians and whites: to kill the Indians or put an end to their Indian ways of life. Officials began a policy to encourage the Indians to give up their culture, or assimilate. The policy set up a system that would force Indians to give up most of their land and live on only the small portion that would be reserved for them. Indians were to move to these reservations and remain there, where they would live in small groups, separated from other Indians and unable to practice their traditional ways of life. Officials believed that they would soon see that the way of life practiced by white Americans was far better and would then readily give up their old ways to adopt the new. The government agency in charge of handling matters concerning Indians, the Bureau of Indian Affairs (BIA), sent agents to the reservations to teach the Indians how to farm and live like white people. Missionaries and Indian agents taught the Indians about Christianity and the English language.

Across the West, Indians were forced to move onto reservations. Texas grudgingly gave up two small parcels of land in the north along the Brazos River and the Clear Fork of the Brazos. These two reservations were too small to support all the Indians in Texas, yet the tribes were expected to move there nonetheless. Most did not. The remnants of the various Caddoan tribes

One of a series of forts built in Texas by the U.S. government to protect white settlers from Indian raids.

BIA agent Robert Neighbors and his wife. Neighbors was killed by a Texan for his attempts to prevent the slaughter of Indians by whites in the state.

were placed on one reservation, and a group of southern Comanche was convinced to go to the other. Some Penateka moved onto the Comanche reservation, but most refused to settle down on the small piece of ground along the Brazos River and continued to live on the Comanchería as they had for centuries.

In 1857 and 1858 Comanche raids in Texas increased. The line of forts constructed to protect Texans had made it difficult and dangerous for the Comanche to go south to Mexico. Instead of discouraging Comanche raids, however, the barrier that kept them away from Mexico caused them to focus their raids on Texas. Unfortunately for the Comanche, they now had to contend with not only the experienced Texas Indian fighter units but also soldiers of the U. S. Army, who pursued the Indian raiders into the interior and attacked them in the north, south, east, and west. By the late 1850s the Comanche, surrounded by numerous, powerful, and well-armed enemies, were not safe anywhere in the Comanchería.

Texas settlers, unable to find the raiding Comanche, frequently attacked and robbed the Indians living peacefully on the Texas reservations. Attacks became so severe that the BIA's agent for the Texas Indians, Robert Neighbors, became convinced that unless the Indians were moved they would be destroyed. He convinced the federal government to provide land for them outside of Texas, and in July 1859 moved them north across the Red River into Indian Territory. The Indians were forced to move quickly and were unable to take all of their possessions. After moving the Indians north, Neighbors returned to Texas to complete his report on their removal. He stopped briefly at Belknap, and when he criticized the attacks on the peaceful Indians a Texan murdered him.

Only 384 Comanches were among the Indians moved north by Neighbors. Those Comanche living off the reservation continued to be attacked by the Texans and federal troops and were in deplorable condition by 1860. Fortunately for the Comanche the Civil War broke out in 1861. Union and Texas soldiers were busy fighting each other.

There were fewer troops available to chase the Comanche, so most of the raids on the Comanchería ended during the war. Both Northern and Southern forces approached the Comanche and asked for peace. The Comanche talked to both and for the most part did not take sides in the conflict. They enjoyed the brief peace and impartially stole horses and mules from both the Union and the Confederacy.

In 1864, responding to increased Kiowa raids on the Santa Fe trail, the federal government sent troops into the Comanchería. Army officials in New Mexico turned to an experienced frontier fighter and settler, Christopher ("Kit") Carson, to lead this army. He had spent most of his life in the Southwest as a hunter, trapper, guide, and soldier and was very familiar with both the land and its people. Carson and his soldiers entered the Comanchería and attacked two large camps of Kiowa and Comanche on the Canadian River near the site of an old trading post known as Adobe Walls. Carson did little damage for he was clearly outnumbered,

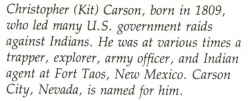

Christopher (Kit) Carson, born in 1809, who led many U.S. government raids against Indians. He was at various times a trapper, explorer, army officer, and Indian agent at Fort Taos, New Mexico. Carson City, Nevada, is named for him.

but he had succeeded in penetrating the Comanchería and attacking the Comanche and Kiowa where they had always been safe before. Their control of their land would soon be over. ▲

The Great Medicine Lodge, on Medicine Lodge Creek, drawn for Frank Leslie's Illustrated Newspaper in 1867. Peace commissioners came from Washington, D.C., to Kansas to meet with leaders of the Comanche and other Plains Indian tribes.

LIFE
AFTER
DEFEAT

With the end of the Civil War in 1865 the United States government wanted to end the violence on the southern Plains. In the fall of that year federal representatives met with several bands of Comanche, Kiowa, Cheyenne, and Arapaho on the Little Arkansas River. The Comanche and the Kiowa promised to stop attacking white settlements and traders on the Santa Fe Trail and to return all white captives. In return, the United States drew up boundaries for Comanche and Kiowa territory that they promised to protect.

The land promised in 1865 was a reduction of the Comanchería, but included most of present-day west Texas and western Oklahoma. Unfortunately for the Comanche, the Texans refused to give up any land for the Indians. Once again United States troops moved into forts along the boundaries of the Comanchería, ready to pursue and punish any Comanche raider, but un-willing to stop any white settlers from moving onto Comanche soil.

As whites continued to move onto the Comanche lands, the Comanche continued to attack them and steal their cattle and horses. While the Comanche fought on the southern Plains, their neighbors and friends to the north, the Cheyenne and Arapaho, were resisting white pressures on the central Plains. In another effort to end the violence on the central and southern Plains, the federal government in 1867 sent a peace commission consisting of political and military leaders to meet with the Indians. The peace commission met with several thousand Comanche, Kiowa, Kiowa-Apache, Cheyenne, and Arapaho Indians gathered at Medicine Lodge Creek. Kiowa and Comanche spokesmen talked with the government agents. Ten Bears, a Yamparika leader who spoke for the Penateka, Yamparika, and Nokoni divisions, pleaded for

Yamparika Comanche leader Ten Bears, photographed in 1872. Ten Bears, who represented the Comanche tribe in Washington on several occasions, spoke eloquently of the Indians' way of life at the Medicine Lodge council.

the Indians to be left alone. Ten Bears had gone to Washington several years before and had seen the might of the government. His words were eloquent.

> My people have never first drawn a bow or fired a gun against the whites. There has been trouble between us, and my young men have danced the war dance. But it was not begun by us. It was you who sent out the first soldier and we who sent out the second. . . . If the Texans had kept out of our country, there might have been peace.
>
> But that which you now say we must live on is too small. The Texans have taken away the places where the grass grew the thickest and the timber was the best. Had we kept that, we

might have done the things you ask. But it is too late. The white man has the country which we loved, and we only wish to wander on the prairie until we die.

The peace commission listened to Ten Bears and also to Satanta, the Kiowa leader, and once again promised to protect Comanche and Kiowa land and keep the whites out. The government sharply reduced the amount of land guaranteed to the Comanche and created for them a reservation not within the state of Texas but completely within Indian Territory. The new Comanche land was bounded on the south by the Red River and on the north by the Washita River. Lines drawn from two points on the Washita south to the Red formed the western and eastern boundaries of this reservation.

This small corner of Indian Territory consisted of only 5,546 square miles and left out all the best hunting land, which was in Texas. The Comanche continued to consider all the land south of the Arkansas River theirs. Although 10 leaders signed the agreement, only a few bands agreed to move to the new reservation. The Quahadi in the west and the Kotsoteka had not been present at the Medicine Lodge meeting and refused to leave the Plains to move to the reservation.

It was clear to federal officials that as long as Indians remained hunters they would not stay on reservations. Officials believed that if the Comanche would settle down and become farmers they would cease raiding and problems with them would be over. They began a program to convert the Comanche from nomadic hunters to sedentary farmers, but this program was never successful. The Comanche had been nomadic hunters for more than 200 years. It was a way of life that they loved. It would not be easy to get them to give it up for a way of life they had no experience with. Ten Bears's words at Medicine Lodge express it best.

> I was born upon the prairie, where the wind blew free and there was nothing to break the light of the sun. I was born where there were no enclosures and where everything drew a free breath. I want to die there and not remain within walls. I know every stream and every wood between the Rio Grande and the Arkansas. I have hunted and lived over that country. I live like my fathers before me and like them I lived happily.

To a people who had long been on the move hunting buffalo, the settled life on the reservation was not attractive. Unable to hunt the buffalo, the Comanche had no hides from which to make their tipi covers and warm clothing. They became dependent on the government for woven cloth—canvas for their tipis and calico for their clothing. The Comanche did not know how to farm and, more important, did not want to. Moreover, their new reservation was poor farming country. The few Comanche who did farm there had little success. The government had to feed

the Comanche or they would leave the reservation to hunt, which would delay their transformation into farmers and lead to violence with whites. In 1869 the government established Fort Sill along Cache Creek (near present-day Lawton) on the Comanche reservation to keep a close eye on them.

Those Comanche who refused to go to the reservation continued their old way of life. They continued to follow the buffalo and hunt, although by the late 1860s the herds became smaller and smaller as more and more people hunted them. They also continued to

A Comanche family in front of their tipi on their reservation in Oklahoma territory. Because there were no longer any buffalo to hunt, the Indians made their tipis of canvas instead of hides.

raid, and more troops were sent against them. U. S. soldiers from forts in New Mexico, Texas, and Indian Territory constantly tried to drive the Comanche onto the reservation. The presence of soldiers made it difficult for the Comanche to raid as successfully as they had formerly, but as long as conditions off the reservation were better than those on the reservation, the Kotsoteka and the Quahadi refused to move there.

By 1873 conditions on the reservation had deteriorated. Congress was reluctant to provide enough money to provide properly for the Indians and bad weather kept supply wagons from reaching Fort Sill. The BIA agent for the Comanche cut back on their food rations and many people were forced to butcher their mules and horses to feed their families. Others left the reservation and joined the bands that continued to hunt.

In 1873, Ishatai, a Quahadi Comanche, began preaching to his people on the Plains about a way to return to the good times of the past. Ishatai told his people that he had ascended into the heavens and spoken with the Great Spirit. The Great Spirit told him to gather the Comanche and lead them in a Sun Dance. The Comanche had never before practiced the Sun Dance, but the desperate circumstances of 1873–74, when the buffalo were almost gone, convinced them to listen to Ishatai. They agreed to perform a Sun Dance to gain the favor of the Great Spirit and gather its powers. Ishatai led the Comanche in their first Sun Dance. When

Comanche Chief Quanah Parker with two of his wives, Pi uuh (left) and So hnee (right), standing on the front porch of the Parker home near Craterville, Oklahoma.

it was over, he told them they must go out to drive the whites from the southern Plains. He claimed that he could protect his followers from the white men's bullets, and that after they had driven the whites away the buffalo would come back. Confident that they had the protection of Ishatai's spiritual power, a large contingent of Comanche, Kiowa, and Cheyenne set out to drive the whites from the land.

They chose to begin their attack on a small trading post on the Canadian River, near the site of Kit Carson's attack in 1864. Adobe Walls was a small outpost made up of several adobe and sod buildings where white buffalo hunters gathered. At the Medicine Lodge meeting the government had promised to keep buffalo hunters north of the Arkansas, but it had not been able to keep them from going further west. Inventors in eastern states had created a new process to convert buffalo hides into a tough leather that was used to make conveyor belts for factories. As the nation rapidly industrialized in the years following the Civil War, this new market for buffalo hides became quite large. To provide hides for eastern factories, hundreds of hunters went west, crossing the Arkansas and killing thousands of buffalo on the southern Plains. They killed thousands of buffalo that the Comanche and the Kiowa believed belonged to them.

The Comanche, Kiowa, and Cheyenne planned a dawn attack on the trading post at Adobe Walls to surprise the hunters. Unfortunately for the Indians, the hunters had spent most of the night repairing a roof beam in one of the buildings. Instead of surprising a sleeping camp, the Indian war party confronted a wide-awake group of hunters armed with large, powerful, and accurate buffalo-hunting rifles. The hunters stayed behind the adobe walls and easily drove off the attacking Indians. Although the Comanche and Kiowa outnumbered the hunters, it became clear that Ishatai's power was not strong enough to defeat the whites. After several unsuccessful charges against the walls and the deadly guns,

the Indians gave up and by late afternoon most of them had drifted away. This fiasco at Adobe Walls would not end the violence, but it did end the Indians' belief in help from the Sun Dance.

The Comanche continued to raid that summer, but they were pursued by well-armed soldiers who invaded the Comanchería from all sides. Troops from Fort Union in New Mexico, Fort Sill in Indian Territory, and Fort Concho in Texas went after the Comanche. In the summer of 1874 soldiers were sent out with orders to drive the Comanche and Kiowa onto the reservation or kill them. Throughout the summer the Indians were attacked by the soldiers. In October Colonel Ranald Mackenzie surprised a large group of Quahadi Comanche camped in Palo Duro Canyon. Mackenzie attacked and his men set fire to the Comanche camp, destroying their tipis, clothing, and food. Most of the Comanche escaped, but Mackenzie's men killed more than 1,500 horses that the Indians had abandoned as they fled the fire and destruction.

Hounded on all sides in the summer and fall of 1874, the Comanche were left in a weakened condition as winter began. Many had no horses, little food, and inadequate shelter. Now even the grim conditions on the reservation seemed better than those out on the Plains. Many Comanche, in order to escape the soldiers and the hunger of a Plains winter, moved to the reservation voluntarily. More came reluctantly, driven by the soldiers. Those who stayed on the Plains had a cold and hungry winter. By the spring of 1875 most had reported to the reservation.

One Quahadi band alone remained on the Plains. In May 1875 Mackenzie sent word to them to come in to the reservation or face attack. The Quahadi broke their camps on top of the breaks of the Llano Estacado and headed for the reservation. On June 2 their leader, Quanah Parker, arrived with his people at the reservation.

Colonel Mackenzie would come to like Parker, the son of Peta Nocona, a Quahadi leader, and Cynthia Ann Parker, a white woman. She had been captured as a child during one of the first Comanche attacks on the Anglo-Texas frontier in 1836. Quanah had become an outstanding warrior among the Quahadi, and was in his twenties when he surrendered his band. Once on the reservation he quickly gained power and influence among Comanche from other bands. The Quahadi leader was apparently willing to cooperate and compromise. He accepted change on some issues but used his power to protect Comanche traditional practices that were important to his people. An extremely intelligent and skillful man, he operated successfully in both the Comanche and white worlds and eventually became the most powerful Comanche leader on the reservation.

Since 1700 the Comanche had roamed the southern Plains, free and independent. In 1875, with the surrender of Quanah Parker's band, Comanche power on the southern Plains came to an end. Now there were no Comanche still living as nomadic hunters. They began a new way of life on the reservation.

When the Comanche arrived on the reservation some of their leaders were briefly imprisoned in the ice house at Fort Sill, and 10 were sent to Fort Marion, Florida. Overall, few Comanche were imprisoned, but all were forced to remain on the reservation, which they shared with the Kiowa and Kiowa-Apache. For several years after their 1875 surrender some left the reservation to hunt buffalo in the summer. Most stayed at home, for after 1875 few buffalo were left on the Plains. The Comanche effectively became prisoners on their reservation. Their only food came from the government, and they could receive it only on the reservation.

The federal government worked through the BIA to get the Comanche to change, to become farmers and behave in all ways like members of white society. BIA officials tried diligently to destroy their culture and to replace the Comanche language, religion, values, economy, and way of life with English, Christianity, capitalism, and agriculture. The Comanche, however, felt they had changed quite enough already. They were satisfied to remain Comanche. Their military defeat and the destruction of the buffalo had forced them to change their economic system and the place where they lived. Now they fought to defend their culture as they had fought to defend their homeland.

The BIA sent agents to live among the Comanche to teach the Plains hunters how to become Plains farmers, but the agents had little success. The Comanche wanted only to hunt, but the whites had massacred the buffalo and now denied them the right to leave the reservation and hunt. Because the government refused to let them feed themselves in the only way they knew, and because they had given the United States millions of acres of land, they thought it was only fair that the government should at least provide food for them. In the next 112 years, the Comanche would continue to resist change, and when pushed would accept it largely on their terms.

The few Comanche who were willing to try farming had to cope with the poor soil and semiarid climate of southwestern Indian Territory. Droughts were common, and Comanche ponies were not strong enough to pull plows through the thick sod. This lack of success made farming even less appealing to the Comanche.

In addition to the cultural resistance of the Comanche to farming and the difficulties of farming in the dry area, the Comanche agents required the heads of all Comanche families to come in person to the agency to pick up their food rations once a week. Few Comanche lived near the agency and requiring them to come in once a week was the

Comanche, Cheyenne, and Kiowa prisoners at Fort Marion in St. Augustine, Florida, photographed in 1875. These tribal leaders were imprisoned to prevent them from influencing the people on the reservation to maintain their traditional way of life.

COMANCHE AND KIOWA LAND CESSIONS

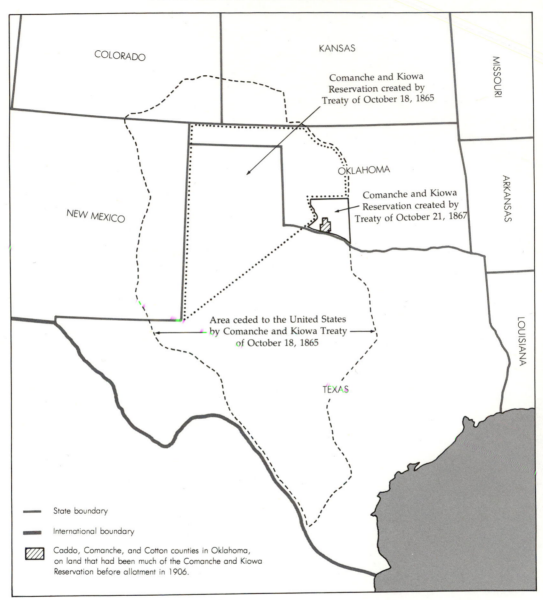

KANSAS

COLORADO

MISSOURI

Comanche and Kiowa
Reservation created by
Treaty of October 18, 1865

OKLAHOMA

ARKANSAS

Comanche and Kiowa
Reservation created by
Treaty of October 21, 1867

NEW MEXICO

LOUISIANA

Area ceded to the United States
by Comanche and Kiowa Treaty
of October 18, 1865

TEXAS

State boundary

International boundary

Caddo, Comanche, and Cotton counties in Oklahoma,
on land that had been much of the Comanche and Kiowa
Reservation before allotment in 1906.

agent's way of keeping a close eye on them. This trip to the agency usually took several days, and it was difficult to farm when one was away three days a week to get the family's rations.

The Comanche reservation was covered with the thick grass that had once supported the buffalo, and it was ideal for raising horses and other livestock. Although most of their horses had been taken from them by the army, some herds remained. Texas horse thieves, however, began to cross the Red River to steal Comanche horses and mules and drive them back to Texas. The federal government did not try to recover the Indians' livestock and would not allow them to leave the reservation to do it for themselves. When the Comanche pursued the thieves into Texas they were punished for leaving the reservation. At times Texas Rangers killed any Comanches they discovered in Texas. In 1880, Congress made it illegal for the Comanche to enter the state of Texas. Texans continued to enter the Comanche reservation and steal horses and mules.

While some Texans were stealing Comanche livestock others began stealing Comanche natural resources. Once the Indians were confined to the reservation Texas ranchers began illegally using the reservation land for pasture. Some ranchers drove their cattle onto the Comanche reservation and sometimes built corrals and camps on Comanche land. Others frequently drove their cattle across reservation land and used Comanche grass and water.

The Comanche showed little interest in raising cattle, and the government initially showed little interest in purchasing cattle for them. In time the Comanche agent purchased some cattle for them but when the agency cut back food rations to save money the Comanche butchered their cattle to feed their people. The first 10 years of reservation life were hungry years for the Coman-

che: With little meat and only the meager government rations to live on, they suffered greatly. There was never enough food for them and with the poor diet many sickened and died. There was only one doctor in the area and he had to serve several reservations with more than 4,000 Indians. Forced to live in contact with each other and outsiders, the Comanche, Kiowa, and Kiowa-Apache were particularly susceptible to the spread of epidemic diseases. Malaria came every summer, and the Comanche suffered and died from measles, smallpox, and bronchial infections as well.

BIA agents continued to work to change the Comanche. To break up their bands, agents encouraged them to live apart in single family dwellings and discouraged group encampments. Agents tried to convince them to give up their tipis and constructed wooden frame houses for them to live in. The houses were not as comfortable or as warm as the tipis, and the Comanche continued to live in their tipis erected next to their frame houses.

Agents also worked to destroy the Comanche political structure. They actively promoted those Comanche who cooperated with the program of change and ignored those leaders who resisted change. To take power away from the old band leaders, agents refused to allow them to pass out food and supplies to their people and insisted on giving supplies out themselves. This severely weakened the band leaders, for much of their power had rested on their ability to distribute food and other goods to the individual families in their bands.

Texas ranchers wanted to use the rich grasslands of the Comanche reservation, especially those lying just north of the Red River. They had used the land illegally for years, but now several of the ranchers were willing to lease the pastureland and pay the Comanche for its use. They approached Quanah and two other influential Comanches, Ishatai and Permansu, and asked them for their help with the leases. In 1884, Quanah and Permansu went to Washington with some of the ranchers and tried to convince the commissioner of Indian affairs to approve the pasture leases. Although unable to get a formal approval, Quanah and the ranchers convinced the reservation agent to accept leases for six cents an acre per year from several of the ranchers without formal permission. This amount was an outrageous bargain for the ranchers. The money, known as the grass payment, initially provided only about $20 per person every year. In time, with official approval, the Comanche leased more land and the grass payments became an important source of revenue. Although they provided some cash for the Indians, the pasture leases actually kept them from developing their own livestock operations because they leased most of their lands to the white ranchers.

Christian missionaries established churches and schools on the reservation and attempted to lure Comanche children to their schools. The BIA also established schools on the reservation in order to teach the ways of the majority of Americans to the children. The Comanche, however, were not interested in sending their children to these schools. From their point of view, the schools had little to offer. They taught Indian children the rules of croquet and baseball; boys were taught elementary bookkeeping and girls were taught to iron clothing, set tables, and address party invitations. These skills had no practical application to Comanche life. The Comanche recognized that the schools were intended to transform their culture, through their children, into that of the white world, and they were not enthusiastic about this prospect. They refused to surrender their children to the whites, and so the schools were not well attended. To pressure the Comanche, agents refused to give families food until they brought their children to school.

Indian agents believed that it would be easier to change the children by removing them from their Comanche families and environment, and many children were taken from their parents and sent away to boarding schools. Some were sent as far away as the Carlisle Indian School in Pennsylvania. Because the BIA wanted to keep them away from the influence of their Indian families, many children were not allowed to return home for years. Children between the ages of 10 and 16 were forced to stay at boarding schools for three to five years. The Comanche, reluctant to have their children go away for several years and come back strangers to their way of life, resisted sending their children to these schools. They knew that Indian children were robbed of their language and culture and were strictly disciplined at the schools. Moreover, the schools were not healthy places, and children often sickened and died there. At both the mission schools and the bureau schools, Comanche children were told that their traditional way of life was wrong and bad, and teachers tried to substitute the language, values, and world views of the white system. Comanche parents won: They did not consistently send their children to school, and those children who attended remained skeptical about the white system. Comanche children defended their language and culture as tena-ciously as their grandparents and parents had defended the Comanchería.

In the face of such a massive attack on their culture, the Comanche showed a tremendous amount of strength. Despite all the efforts of government agents, school teachers, and missionaries, they remained true to their culture. They remained apart and distinct, changing only as much as they had to in order to survive, but they did not give up their culture. They had been forced to give up their wandering, hunting life on the southern Plains, but they remained Comanche.

On the reservation, the Comanche abandoned many of their old guardian spirits and adopted a new religion based on the use of peyote, a part of a cactus that grows in south Texas and Mexico. Peyote is a nonaddictive drug

The Comanche camp at Cache Creek Mission, near Fort Sill, Oklahoma, photographed in 1899. Although wood frame houses were built for them, the Indians preferred to live in their tipis. The women are wearing dresses made from government-issue cloth.

Comanche practitioners of the peyote religion. The group includes Quanah Parker (seated, second from left) and two of his wives, So hnee (standing on left) and Tonicy (standing, second from left), photographed in 1893. Parker was instrumental in gaining federal approval of peyote use despite the attempts of Christian missionaries to have it banned.

that produces mild hallucinations, a sense of harmony with the universe, and feelings of euphoria among users. It often acts as a sedative. Indians in Mexico had used peyote for centuries, and the Comanche learned about its use from the Apache. As early as the 1850s a few of the Comanche had begun taking peyote on special occasions to seek visions. After they moved to the reservation, they began actively to use peyote in their religious practices.

Peyotism was a group religion, and the Comanche who had lived in groups before they were forced apart on the reservation welcomed the opportunity to gather together, to take peyote, sing sacred songs, and pray together. The Comanche taught other people about peyote, and its use spread. The peyote religion did not solve all of their problems, but it did provide spiritual help and solace for a people forced to give up a way of life so dear to them.

The Comanche and other Indian people were harassed by Christian missionaries and the BIA agents for using peyote, but they continued to use it and pray with it. Fortunately for the Comanche, Quanah Parker was among those who practiced the peyote religion, and his support helped to protect it from attacks by government agents. He cooperated with the government by sending his children to government schools and in many other ways, but he refused to give up peyote. Agents needed his support, so they were reluctant to challenge him on peyote and expressed only token disapproval of it. In 1918 the state of Oklahoma finally legalized the use of peyote for Indian people practicing their religion. Today many Comanche remain loyal peyotists, and some are members of the Native American Church, which combines elements of Christianity with Indian beliefs, using peyote as their sacrament.

In 1890 the Comanche heard of a new religion taught by Wovoka, a Paiute Indian spiritual leader. He had a religious experience or vision and began preaching a new religion known as the Ghost Dance. Wovoka told the Indians of the West that if they lived correctly and danced the Ghost Dance, the dead would return to life, the buffalo would come back to the Plains, and the whites would go away. The Indians would not have to resort to violence to drive the whites away; all they had to do was dance the Ghost Dance and live right. Some of the northern Comanche began dancing the Ghost Dance in the back country of the reservation. Among the Sioux on the northern Plains, agents had tried to halt the dance, and violence had erupted at Wounded Knee in December 1890. On the southern Plains, however, agents did not interfere, perhaps because few Comanche danced

the Ghost Dance. The Comanche had followed Ishatai's failed vision in 1874, and the failure at Adobe Walls perhaps made the Comanche a little suspicious of other visionaries. Peyote was already providing spiritual answers for them, and most were not caught up in the message of Wovoka.

The Comanche were able to resist the Christians and the Ghost Dancers, but they were unable to stop the growing demand for their land. Whites believed that the Indians were not using their lands and demanded that the government take it from them so whites could settle and farm on it. Convinced that Indians would remain Indians as long as they lived communally, and believing that private land ownership would hasten the Indians' adoption of the mainstream culture, in 1887 Congress passed the General Allotment Act, also known as the Dawes Act. It gave the president the power to divide the tribally held reservation lands and allot (assign) land to individual Indians. If any Indians refused to select individual homesteads, the government would do it for them. Land would no longer be held communally. After the Indians accepted their individual homesteads they would be granted U.S. citizenship.

The Comanche, like many other tribes, resisted allotment. Like most others, their resistance would prove to be futile. ▲

Vincent Myers, a Comanche who won the 1960 U.S. Interior Department Award for his farming efforts.

A CENTURY
ON THE
LAND

Most Indians did not want allot-ment—they wanted to continue to hold their land communally. They had seen the government take more and more of their territory, and it seemed to most of them that the Dawes Act was an at-tempt to take their last bit of land. The Dawes Act granted 160 acres of land to the head of every family, 80 acres to other adult Indians and orphans under 18 years of age, and 40 acres to all oth-ers. After granting individual Indians their plots of land, the government would sell all unallotted land, and the funds from the sales were to be placed in the U. S. Treasury to be used for the Indians.

The General Allotment Act would change the Indians' legal status and tribal organization as well as their eco-nomic situation. To protect Indian people from those who might take ad-vantage of them, the Dawes Act created a special legal status for them. Their land was to be held in trust by the gov-ernment and could not be sold for 25 years. The government would serve as a guardian to supervise the Indians' le-gal and economic affairs. Indian people were thus considered legally incompe-tent to transact business for themselves.

Allotment opened Indian lands to white settlement. After assigning the Indians their individual plots there were millions of acres left over. This "surplus" land was sold by the govern-ment, and through the Dawes Act American Indians lost more than 102 million acres of land.

The Comanche did not want to sell any of their land and refused to accept allotment. Tribes east of them were forced to accept allotment first, and by 1889, two million acres of Indian Ter-ritory were opened up to white settlers. Thousands poured into the region and took Indian land both legally and ille-gally. Those whites who sought land in

Indian Territory were known as boomers (for the land boom in which they were participating), and those who refused to wait until the government had purchased the land and moved onto it illegally were known as sooners (they occupied the land sooner than they should have). Both boomers and sooners pressured the Indians for their land.

The Comanche did not want to sell, and they were supported by the ranchers who leased grasslands from them. The Texas ranchers, who enjoyed vast leases and low rates, had a bargain and wanted to keep it. They knew that once the Comanche and Kiowa land was divided and sold they could no longer graze their cattle there. So the cowboys and the Indians worked together to fight allotment on the Comanche, Kiowa, and Kiowa-Apache Reservation.

According to the Medicine Lodge Treaty of 1867, any sale of Comanche, Kiowa, and Kiowa-Apache land was supposed to be approved by three-fourths of the men of those tribes. In September 1892 a government commission led by David H. Jerome came to the Comanche, Kiowa, and Kiowa-Apache Reservation and met with the Indians several times that fall. The Indians were not eager to accept allotment, and they tried to delay the commission's work, but the Jerome Commission pressured them to approve the proposed land transfer. To gain Indian support, they promised to give each Comanche, adults and children alike, 160 acres of land and to try to realize $2 million for them from the sale of any land left over after allotment. They also promised to distribute some of the proceeds in cash. If the Comanche did not accept this offer, the Jerome Commission threatened to insist on the provisions of the Dawes Act: 160 acres for the head of a family only and 80 acres or less for all others, with none of the proceeds from the sale of surplus land going directly to the Indians.

This threat to rely on the terms of the Dawes Act was a powerful argument for the approval of the Jerome Agreement. To further ensure that the Indians on the Comanche, Kiowa, and Kiowa-Apache Reservation approved the agreement, the commission included in the document a promise to give 25 influential white people on the reservation an equal share with the Indians of the money and property. Some of these whites were interpreters who had married Indians; others had lived on the reservation for years and had gained the Indians' trust. The commission's offer was intended as a kind of bribe: The whites would get property and money only if they could use their influence to convince the Indians to accept the Jerome Agreement.

Some Comanche realized that allotment was inevitable and tried to strike a better bargain. They argued that 160 acres was insufficient for both dry-land farming and cattle raising. They insisted that unless they received more land they would never be able to become self-supporting and would remain dependent on the federal government.

They asked for 320 acres for each Comanche, Kiowa, and Kiowa-Apache and $2.5 million for the surplus lands.

Using the threat of the Dawes Act and the influence of trusted whites, the Jerome Commission began collecting signatures for their agreement. It is clear that not all of the Indians understood what they were signing. The very idea of allotment and individual ownership was culturally alien to most Indians, whose tradition depended on sharing all resources. Few of the Comanche, Kiowa, and Kiowa-Apache spoke English; the interpreters who translated had a great deal to gain from the agreement and may have misrepresented certain terms to get some people to sign. Many Indians believed that there would be no way to escape allotment and that the Jerome Agreement was the best offer they could get from the government. In time, the Jerome Commission convinced three-fourths of the adult Comanche, Kiowa, and Kiowa-Apache men to sign, as required by the Treaty of Medicine Lodge, and left for Washington with the signed agreement.

The Jerome Agreement was signed in 1892, but Congress did not approve it until 1900. In the meantime, thousands of boomers and sooners moved into Indian Territory. Unwilling to wait for the opening of the reservation, many entered Indian land illegally. Prospectors went into the Wichita Mountains to search for mineral deposits, and sooners settled on reservation lands. Several white communities sprang up just outside of the boundary of the Comanche reservation, and whites entered Comanche land illegally and stole timber for fuel, fencing, and housing.

A crowd in southwestern Oklahoma awaits the start of a U.S. government drawing for the opening of Kiowa, Comanche, Apache, and Wichita lands to white settlement on July 29, 1901. Hundreds of thousands of settlers were brought into Oklahoma by train for the drawing.

*The 1897 delegation of Comanche, Kiowa, and Kiowa-Apache who went to Washington to ar-
gue against the Jerome Agreement. The group is standing in front of the home of Benjamin
Beveridge, at whose hotel Indian delegations stayed. From left in the first row, Comanche
leader Quanah Parker (standing) and his wife Toniny, and Kiowa leaders Apiatan, Apache
John, and Big Looking Glass. Comanche interpreter William Tivis is standing in the middle
row at the far right, and Beveridge and his daughter, are standing on the stairs at the rear.*

They grazed cattle on Comanche grass
and demanded that the Indians move.

Although the Jerome Agreement
had been signed by enough Comanche,
Kiowa, and Kiowa-Apache men to
make it legal and binding, several Indian leaders went to Washington in
1893, 1894, and 1897 to fight the approval of the agreement and tried to
change it. Among them was Quanah
Parker, who asked federal officials to
delay allotment for five years and increase the size of the allotment tracts.
These Indian leaders could not halt allotment, but they did delay it for a time
and were able to save an additional
480,000 acres of land for their people.
This land was to be owned in common

by all three tribes on the reservation. Most of the communally held land was in the south, bordering the Red River, and was leased to Texas ranchers.

In late July 1900, unable to postpone allotment any longer, the Comanche selected their individual homesteads. Most chose land on or near where they were already living. The Kiowa and Kiowa-Apache selected land in the north, and the Comanche picked land in the south. Although the federal officials had worked for years to destroy them, four Comanche bands survived, and when the Comanche chose their homesteads they selected them according to band locations. The Penateka people chose their homesteads generally in the southernmost part of the reservation. The Quahadi band chose homesteads north of the Penateka and west of Fort Sill. The Nokoni picked homesteads north and slightly east of the Quahadi, and north of them the Yamparika chose their individual parcels of land. Although confined on the reservation and forced to own land individually, the Comanche chose to remain with their band kin. They settled in the old patterns of the Comanchería.

After the Indians chose their homesteads the government prepared to open their surplus lands for settlement by the land-hungry whites eager to move onto the reservation. Now there was no land rush into the Comanche, Kiowa, and Kiowa-Apache Reservation, because the government decided to use a lottery to grant land. The surplus land was divided into 13,000 homesteads, for which 165,000 whites had applied. The lottery was held in July 1901, and shortly thereafter whites invaded the Comanchería once again.

After 1901 the communally owned land of the Comanche, Kiowa, and Kiowa-Apache consisted of only 480,000 acres. They continued to lease this land to Texas ranchers, and the grass leases remained profitable. Whites, however, soon demanded that the government take that last portion of land away from the Indians and make it available for settlement. Several bills were introduced in Congress to accomplish this. The Indian agent tried to keep the land for the Indians, arguing that the leases provided more than $100,000 every year for them, and that the proposed bill, which offered a final payment of only $1.50 an acre, would provide only $600,000 in one lump sum. He pointed out that the Comanche could barely survive on the 160-acre homesteads because of the quality of the land, and that although the per capita (per person) grass payments were small, they enabled the Comanche to survive. He feared that the sale of their communal lands would condemn the Comanche, Kiowa, and Kiowa-Apache to lives of dependence and poverty.

Despite the agent's arguments the federal government decided to take the communal lands. In 1906 the government raised the price to $5.00 an acre, transferred $4 million to the tribes' treasury account, and took their land. After September 1906 the Comanche held land only as individuals. Tragically, many lost even their individual homesteads in a very short time.

What had once been known as Indian Territory became the state of Oklahoma in 1907. Many whites living in the state wanted what remained of the Indians' lands. Although the Comanche were finding it difficult to farm or raise cattle on 160 acres of land, Oklahoma politicians tried to convince Congress to reduce the individual Comanche homesteads to just 80 acres. Fortunately for the Comanche, Congress refused to allow Oklahoma to take more of their land and let them keep their small homesteads.

In 1908, however, Congress decided to end the trust status of allotted land belonging to mixed-bloods. These were Indians who had non-Indian ancestors. People such as Quanah Parker, whose mother was white, were given full title to their land and allowed to sell it. Unfortunately, as soon as they gained title to their land most were swindled out of it. Within four years 90 percent of the land granted in title to the mixed-blood Comanche had been sold to whites.

There was still another unfortunate aspect of the 1908 law that exempted the mixed-bloods from the trust provisions of the Dawes Act. Almost all of the full-blood Comanche who held allotments were still considered legally incompetent to manage their affairs. The federal government's guardianship of these Indians and its supervision of other legal matters were transferred to county courts in each state. After 1908 county judges in Cotton, Comanche, and Caddo counties assigned guardians to manage what little property the Comanche had left. Few if any of these

guardians had the Indians' interests at heart, and the Comanche were cheated out of thousands of acres of land and resources. As a result of allotment a group of landless Comanche was created from a people who had controlled millions of acres of land less than 100 years before.

From 1900 to 1936 times were grim indeed for the Comanche in Oklahoma. Those who kept their land struggled to survive as independent farmers and as laborers for white ranchers and farmers. Many struggled on annual incomes of less than $200 per family. Living in poverty, they suffered from poor diets and ill health. In the early 1930s the Comanche were further hurt by the droughts that made much of Oklahoma a dust bowl where nothing would grow, as well as by the economic depression that affected the entire nation. These brought even more hunger and suffering to them.

With the inauguration of President Franklin Roosevelt in 1933 came the promise of a "New Deal" that would bring improved economic conditions. The Wheeler-Howard Act of 1934 was the cornerstone of the federal policy that came to be known as the Indian New Deal. But that act, which provided so much help for other Indians, did not apply to any Indians in Oklahoma. The following year Congress solved that omission by passing the Oklahoma Indian Welfare Act, which allocated funds for health care and education specifically to the Indians of that state.

An important part of all the New Deal Indian programs was that they were administered with respect and regard for Indian people and their way of life. Indians were allowed to determine for themselves what kind of life they would lead. They were guaranteed freedom of religion. The federal government ended programs forcing the Indians to adopt white people's culture, and it reestablished Indian schools. The new federal legislation also provided a means by which tribal organizations could be set up. The Comanche had belonged to the council established in the 1890s known as the Comanche, Kiowa, Kiowa-Apache Business Council. After allotment there was little for the business council to do. After the passage of the Oklahoma Indian Welfare Act, the Comanche, Kiowa, Kiowa-Apache Business Council was reorganized and recognized as the official tribal government for the three tribes.

With the outbreak of World War II many Comanche young men volunteered and fought for the United States, as they had a generation earlier in World War I. After the war these men came home with new attitudes about the world and new views of themselves. Some refused to remain in Oklahoma and accept second-class citizenship and moved from Oklahoma to make their lives in California and elsewhere.

After the war, Congress, intent on cutting government spending, decided to end its special relationship with Indian people. This new policy, known as termination, threatened many Indians with the loss of support from various government programs. It was less

Comanche Clifford Martinez, working as a machinist for Douglas Aircraft Co. during World War II. Many Indians took part in the war effort, serving in the military as well as working in defense industries.

a threat to the Comanche than to some other tribes because the government had already taken their land away from them. But without federal help most of the Comanche could not afford adequate health care. With the closing of the BIA schools, Comanche children had to attend local public schools. Without federal help, few could afford to continue their education at vocational schools or colleges. Fortunately for the Comanche, the drive for termination weakened in the early 1960s, and they did not lose their relationship with the federal government.

In 1966 the Comanche left the Comanche, Kiowa, Kiowa-Apache Business Council because they claimed that

Comanche tribal housing commissioners and representatives from the U.S. Department of Housing and Urban Development at the 1987 ground-breaking ceremony for a housing complex that will provide homes for 50 Indian families just north of Comanche Tribal Headquarters in Lawton, Oklahoma.

the Kiowa and the Kiowa-Apache worked together against them. The Comanche tribe wrote its own tribal constitution and created a Comanche Business Committee, whose members are elected, to handle financial affairs for the tribe. The Comanche constitution also provides for a Tribal Council composed of all Comanche tribal members who are 18 years or older. The Comanche Tribe, in order to help improve economic opportunities, established a meat-packing plant and a leather tannery to process cowhides.

Comanche young men served in the war in Vietnam. Some were drafted and many enlisted. The Comanche, who have retained their respect for military service, created the Comanche Indian Veterans Association, which honors all veterans and conducts powwows. In 1972 a group of Vietnam veterans established the Little Ponies, which organizes and conducts powwows and keeps Comanche traditions alive today.

But the Comanche and other Indians in Oklahoma continue to suffer from racism and poverty. Conditions have improved dramatically from what they were in the 19th century, but there remains a great deal to be done. Local school boards show little respect for Indians and their culture and continue to try to convert their children to the culture of white Americans. BIA schools have reopened but are woefully understaffed and poorly maintained. Students in Indian vocational schools may still receive training for jobs that do not exist on or near their homes. Unemployment remains high for most Indians. There is evidence of many kinds of discrimination against Indians: A 1977 survey of Indian living conditions in six western Oklahoma counties found that Indians were more frequently arrested and jailed than whites for similar offenses, and that during arrests more force was used on Indians than on whites. The survey also showed that the local public schools drove Indian children away by trying to force them to deny their culture.

Many Comanche remain in Cotton, Caddo, and Comanche counties in southwestern Oklahoma. The tribal headquarters is located in Medicine Park just north of Fort Sill. The Comanche have maintained their band relationships. The Penateka live in the south in Cotton County around Walters, Oklahoma, whereas the Quahadi live in western Comanche County. The Nokoni and Yamparika live north of Medicine Park and remain the most traditional of all the Comanche.

The Comanche function in the modern, mainstream white world yet continue to preserve tribal traditions. Although English is the primary language of most Comanche, their original language survives. Some Comanche still ranch and some farm their lands. Allotted land became subdivided through inheritance among members of large families, and only small parcels are now owned by each individual. These are often not large enough to ranch or farm. Some Comanche are employed in the oilfields of Texas and Oklahoma, while others hold jobs in communities as skilled and professional workers—machinists, electricians, certified public accountants, and teachers. Some work for the federal government as employees of the BIA or on nearby military installations such as Fort Sill and Tinker Air Force Base. Many young Comanche, upon graduating from high school, join the military service, both to receive skilled training and because military service is still honored as part of their warrior tradition.

The Comanche Tribe, the Comanche Indian Veterans Association, and the Little Ponies all sponsor tribal gatherings several times during the year. In the summer the Comanche come together all over Comanche country to camp and dance. They meet at Anadarko for the large powwow that draws

LaDonna Harris, a Comanche from Lawton, Oklahoma, founded Americans for Indian Opportunity in 1970. The organization advocates natural resource management, improved environmental quality, and efforts toward tribal self-government. Harris served on presidential commissions in the Johnson, Ford, and Carter administrations.

Indians of many tribes, and in Walters, Oklahoma, for the annual Comanche Homecoming every August.

Some Comanche still practice peyotism; others are members of other Christian churches. Despite years of pressure to change, many Comanche continue to dance, pray, and maintain their cultural heritage together. They retain their separate and distinct outlook on life. The creation of the Little Ponies in 1972 is evidence of their steadfast hold on their heritage. They are no longer the masters of the southern Plains, but they have fought to remain what they are—the Comanche. ▲

BIBLIOGRAPHY

Fehrenbach, T. R. *Comanches: The Destruction of a People*. New York: Knopf, 1974.

Gibson, Arrell Morgan. *The American Indian: Prehistory to Present*. Lexington, MA: Heath, 1980.

John, Elizabeth A. H. *Storms Brewed in Other Men's Worlds: The Confrontation of Indian, Spanish, and French in the Southwest, 1540–1795*. College Station, TX: Texas A&M Press, 1975.

Jones, David E. *Sanapia: Comanche Medicine Woman*. New York: Holt, Rinehart and Winston, 1974.

Kenner, Charles. *The Plains Indians and New Mexico*. Norman: University of Oklahoma Press, 1969.

Richardson, Rupert N. *The Comanche Barrier to South Plains Settlement: A Century and a Half of Savage Resistance to the Advancing White Frontier*. Glendale, CA: Arthur H. Clark Company, 1933.

Secoy, Frank. *Changing Military Patterns on the Great Plains*. Monograph of the American Ethnological Society, No. 21. Locust Valley, NY: J. J. Augustin, 1953.

Wallace, Ernest, and E. Adamson Hoebel. *The Comanches: Lords of the Southern Plains*. Norman: University of Oklahoma Press, 1952.

THE COMANCHE AT A GLANCE

TRIBE *Comanche*

CULTURE AREA *Great Plains*

GEOGRAPHY *southern Plains of Texas, eastern New Mexico, western Oklahoma, southeastern Colorado, and southern Kansas*

LINGUISTIC FAMILY *Shoshonean*

CURRENT POPULATION *approximately 8,500*

FIRST CONTACT *Captain Cristobal de la Serna, Spanish, 1705*

FEDERAL STATUS *recognized; reservation in Oklahoma.*

GLOSSARY

adobe A building material or brick made of sun-dried earth and straw.

agent A person appointed by the Bureau of Indian Affairs to supervise U.S. government programs on a reservation and/or in a specific region. After 1908 the title superintendent replaced agent.

allotment U.S. policy, first applied in 1887, to break up tribally owned reservations by assigning individual farms and ranches to Indians. Allotment was intended as much to discourage traditional communal activities as to encourage private farming and assimilate Indians into mainstream American life.

band A territorially based and simply organized group of people who are substantially dependent upon hunting and gathering for subsistence.

breechcloth or *breechclout* A soft piece of hide or cloth, usually worn by American Indian men, wrapped between the legs and held in place by a belt or string around the waist.

Bureau of Indian Affairs (BIA) A U.S. government agency within the Department of the Interior. Originally intended to manage trade and other relations with Indians, the BIA now seeks to develop and implement programs that encourage Indians to manage their own affairs and to improve their educational opportunities and general social and economic well-being.

Carlisle Indian School A federally funded boarding school in Pennsylvania. Young Indians of many tribes who were sent there during the late 19th and early 20th centuries were forced to assimilate into white culture.

Comanchería The Spanish term for the land on which the Comanche lived. The Comanchería was located on the Great Plains in what are now sections of the states of Texas, Colorado, and Oklahoma.

conquistadores The Spanish term for "conquerors"; Spanish soldiers and explorers who invaded Indian lands and subjugated the Indian peoples of southeastern and southwestern North America, Central America and many areas of South America.

coup An honor awarded to a Comanche warrior for an act of great bravery in battle or against an enemy.

culture The learned behavior of humans' nonbiological, socially taught activities; the way of life of a group of people.

Great Plains A flat, dry region in central North America, covered primarily by lush grasslands. The Comanche moved to the Plains in the late 17th century from the Colorado and Wyoming border area.

Indian Territory An area in the south central United States to which the U.S. government wanted to resettle Indians from other regions, especially the eastern states. In 1907, the territory became the state of Oklahoma.

irrigation The routing of water to dry land through ditches, canals, or other means in order to make cultivation possible.

Llano Estacado The Spanish term for the Staked Plains, a raised flat stretch of treeless land extending along most of the Texas–New Mexico border.

mission Religious centers founded in colonized areas by advocates of a particular religion who try to convert nonbelievers to their faith.

nomadic Way of life of human societies that move frequently to follow game and other seasonal food resources and do not have one fixed place to live; the opposite of sedentary.

parfleche French for "rawhide"; also, a folded rectangular container made of rawhide, used for storing dried foods, blankets, and clothing.

peyote A button or growth of the mescal cactus, native to Texas, New Mexico, Arizona, and the northern Mexican states; used as the vehicle or channel of prayer in the Native American Church.

presidio A Spanish frontier military post or fort.

Pueblo A Spanish term for a town or village of certain southwestern Indians; also the name of the group of Indian peoples of the Southwest who inhabited these villages.

removal policy National policy, begun in 1830, calling for the sale of all Indian land in the eastern and southern United States and the migration of Indians from these areas to lands across the Mississippi River. Many Plains Indian peoples, including the Comanche, lost large portions of their lands in order to make room for the tribes that were removed.

reservation or *reserve* A tract of land set aside by treaty for Indian occupation and use.

termination Federal policy to remove Indian tribes from government supervision and Indian lands from trust status, in effect from the late 1940s through the 1960s.

territory A defined region of the United States that is not but may become a state. The government officials of a territory are appointed by the president, but territory residents elect their own legislature.

tipi A conical, portable shelter made of poles and covered with buffalo hides; the principal dwelling of most Plains Indians, including the Comanche.

treaty A contract negotiated between representatives of the United States government or another national government and one or more Indian tribes. Treaties dealt with surrender of political independence, peaceful relations, boundaries, terms of land sales, and related mattters.

tribe A society consisting of several or many separate communities united by kinship, culture, language, and such other social factors as clans, religious organizations, and economic and political institutions.

trust The relationship between the federal government and many Indian tribes, dating from the late 19th century. Government agents managed Indians' business dealings, including land transactions and rights to national resources, because the Indians were considered legally incompetent to manage their own affairs.

INDEX

PICTURE CREDITS

Photos by Adam Anik, Department of Library Services, American Museum of Natural History, page 38 (left: neg. # 2A14680; right: neg. # 2A14679); Americans for Indian Opportunity/Jerry Mesmer 1086, Adams Studio, Inc., page 103; Barker Texas History Center, pages 12, 60; Bettmann Archive, pages 14, 16; Bureau of American Ethnology, Smithsonian Institution, page 41 (neg. # 360.233A); Bureau of Land Management, U.S. Department of the Interior, page 97; Colorado Historical Society, Denver, Colorado, pages 56, 63; Comanche Tribal Headquarters, Lawton, Oklahoma, page 102; Culver Pictures, pages 50, 76; Denver Art Museum, page 47; Daughters of the Republic of Texas Library, San Antonio, Texas, pages 51, 77; The Field Museum of Natural History, Chicago, Illinois, page 68 (top: neg. # A11506C). Fort Sill Museum, Fort Sill, Oklahoma, page 83; The Thomas Gilcrease Institute of Texas Culture, page 87; Photos by Sarah Lewis, pages 66–67; Library of Congress, pages 62, 80; Lowie Museum of Anthropology, page 72 (top, right); Museum of the Great Plains, page 91; Photos courtesy of the Museum of New Mexico, page 26 (neg. # 139987), 79 (neg. # 7151); Museum of Texas Tech University, pages 36, 68 (bottom), 72 (top, left); National Anthropological Archives, Smithsonian Institution, pages 82 (neg. # 1741-a), 92 (neg. # 1778-a), 98 (neg. # 44.453-a); National Archives, page 94; National Archives, Bureau of Indian Affairs Collection, page 101; National Archives of Canada, pages 30 (neg. # C 403), 33 (neg. # C 407); National Collection of Fine Arts, Smithsonian Institution, page 42; National Museum of American Art, Smithsonian Institution, page 34; The New-York Historical Society, page 28; The New York Public Library, Astor and Tilden Foundation, page 19; The New York Public Library, Archives and Rare Books Division, page 75; Panhandle Plains Museum, Canyon, Texas, pages 52, 65, 69 (middle); The Charles M. Russell Museum, page 45; San Antonio Museum Association, page 59; School of American Research, page 40; Texas Memorial Museum, page 78; NAA Smithsonian, pages 69 (top), 70–71, 72 (bottom); U. T. Institute of Texan Cultures at San Antonio, page 74; Walters Art Gallery, pages 15, 20; West Point Museum, page 48; Western History Collections, University of Oklahoma Library, page 84.

Maps (pages 2, 25, 88) by Gary Tong.

WILLARD H. ROLLINGS is assistant professor of history at Southwest Missouri State University. He holds a B.A. and M.A. in history from New Mexico State University, a Ph.D. in history from Texas Tech University, and was a post-doctoral research fellow at the D'Arcy McNickle Center for the History of the American Indian. He is the author of many articles and book chapters on Native American history and the history of the American frontier, including "Multi-sided Frontier: Indians, Frenchmen, Spanish, and Anglos on the Southern Plains" in *New Directions in American History* and "Pueblo Indians: Land and Water" in the *American Indian Culture and Research Journal*. His primary research interest is the ethnohistory of Native Americans of the southern Plains and the Southwest.

FRANK W. PORTER III, general editor of INDIANS OF NORTH AMERICA, is director of the Chelsea House Foundation for American Indian Studies. He holds a B.A., M.A., and Ph.D. from the University of Maryland. He has done extensive research concerning the Indians of Maryland and Delaware and is the author of numerous articles on their history, archaeology, geography, and ethnography. He was formerly director of the Maryland Commission on Indian Affairs and American Indian Research and Resource Institute, Gettysburg, Pennsylvania, and he has received grants from the Delaware Humanities Forum, the Maryland Committee for the Humanities, the Ford Foundation, and the National Endowment for the Humanities, among others. Dr. Porter is the author of *The Bureau of Indian Affairs* in the Chelsea House KNOW YOUR GOVERNMENT series.